BEATRICE SIMON • BARBARA WILDER

Granny Squares
All Shapes and Sizes

Over 50 projects and techniques to give the classic crochet
pattern a whole new look

D1341520

Search Press

800 464 307

KIRKLEES LIBRARIES

First published in Great Britain
in 2014 by
Search Press Limited
Wellwood, North Farm Road, Tunbridge Wells, Kent TN2 3DR

Also published in the United States of America
in 2014 by
Trafalgar Square Books
North Pomfret, Vermont 05053

Originally published in German as *Granny Squares auf andere Art*

Copyright © 2012 frechverlag GmbH, Stuttgart, Germany (www.frechverlag.de)
English translation © 2014 Trafalgar Square Books

This edition is published by arrangement with Claudia Böhme Rights & Literary
Agency, Hannover, Germany (www.agency-boehme.com).

All rights reserved. No part of this book, text, photographs or illustrations may
be reproduced or transmitted in any form or by any means by print, photoprint,
microfilm, microfiche, photocopier, internet or in any way known or as yet
unknown, or stored in a retrieval system, without written permission obtained
beforehand from Search Press.

The instructions and material lists in this book were carefully reviewed by the
author and editor, however, accuracy cannot be guaranteed. The author and
publisher cannot be held liable for errors.

ISBN: 978-1-78221-049-8

Translation by Donna Druchunas
Diagrams: Béatrice Simon (pp. 58-71), Barbara Wilder (pp. 24, 26, 34, 36, 38,
40, 42, 48)
Photography: Barbara Wilder (p. 77); Sabine Münch; Michael Ruder; author
portraits courtesy of Barbara Wilder and Béatrice Simon
Graphic design: Petra Theilfarth

Printed in China

10 9 8 7 6 5 4 3 2 1

CONTENTS

Granny Squares—
All Shapes and Sizes

Who could resist yesterday's popular granny squares, now updated and trendy? Colorful motifs in exciting new shapes and designs invite you to crochet them. Whether you're at the park, on the train, or at your favorite place to hang out and relax, you're certain to see granny-square purses and accessories passing by. Crochet motifs can also be made into beautiful pillows, blankets, stool covers, or placemats for decorating the home. Whatever your taste, you'll be inspired by our modern ideas and fresh projects, all infused with a little whimsy. With these projects, you are guaranteed to be in fashion. We wish you hours and hours of crochet fun!

Easy as Granny Squares

Whatever their shape, just like granny squares, stars, circles, and triangles have one thing in common—they are quick and easy to crochet.

Each of these new "grannies" is visually appealing, but, when joined into pillows, bags, rugs, and fashion accessories, they become the highlights of your decor, making your home shine with splendor. Working these new motifs will give you hours of pleasure.

Each of the new "granny" motifs is worked in the round from the center outward. Following the instructions, given in charts and in written form, you'll master the technique in no time.

Revel in the infinite variations and possible combinations—the motifs and forms can be combined to create endless variety.

● = Slip stitch (sl st)

o = Chain (ch)

× = Double crochet (dc) (US single crochet)

⋎ = Increase by working 2 dc in 1 stitch

⋏ = Decrease by working 2 double crochets together (dc2tog)

⋎₃ = Increase by working 3 dc in 1 stitch

T = Half treble crochet (htr) (US half double)

Ŧ = Treble crochet (tr) (US double)

Ŧ = Double treble crochet (dtr) (US treble)

Ŧ = Triple treble crochet (ttr) (US double treble crochet)

 = Back post quadruple treble crochet (BP quad tr) (US back post triple treble)

○ = Magic ring

 = Beginning half treble crochet cluster (beg htr cluster)

 = Half treble crochet cluster (htr cluster)

 = Beginning 2 treble crochet cluster (beg 2 tr cluster)

 = 2 treble crochet cluster (2 tr cluster)

 = Beginning 3 treble crochet cluster (beg 3 tr cluster)

 = 3 treble crochet cluster (3 tr cluster)

 = Beginning 4 treble crochet cluster (beg 4 tr cluster)

 = 4 treble crochet cluster (4 tr cluster)

 = Tr worked into base of previous stitch

 = Elongated half treble crochet

 = Elongated treble crochet

×ᴺ = Crab stitch (reverse double crochet)

 = Chain space with 6/7/9 chains

⌢ = Petal group from previous round

♡ = 1 Picot

Note: As shown in the charts, the first htr of a round is replaced by ch 2, the first tr by ch 3, and the first dtr by ch 4. Each round is joined at the end with a slip stitch worked into the top of the beginning chain.

Basic Triangle

Ch 4. Join with sl st in the first ch to form a ring.
Rnd 1: Ch 3 (= 1 tr), 3 tr in ring, ch 2, (4 tr in ring, ch 2) twice. Join with sl st in beg ch.
Rnd 2: Ch 4 (= ch 1 + 1 tr), *(3 tr, ch 2, 4 tr) in next ch-sp, ch 1, (4 tr, ch 2, 4 tr) in next ch-sp, ch 1, (4 tr, ch 2, 4 tr) in next ch-sp. Join with sl st in beg ch.
Rnd 3: Join new color with sl st in 2-ch sp, ch 3 (= 1 tr), (3 tr, ch 2, 4 tr) in same ch-sp, ch 1, 4 tr in next ch-sp, ch 1, *(4 tr, ch 2, 4 tr) in next ch-sp, ch 1, 4 tr in next ch-sp, ch 1 rep from * once more. Join with sl st in beg ch.
Rnd 4: Join new color with sl st in 2-ch sp, ch 3 (= 1 tr), (3 tr, ch 2, 4 tr) in same ch-sp, (ch 1, 4 tr in next ch-sp) twice, ch 1, *(4 tr, ch 2, 4 tr) in next ch-sp, (ch 1, 4 tr in next ch-sp) twice, ch 1, rep from * once more. Join with sl st in beg ch.
Rnd 5: Join new color with sl st in 2-ch sp, ch 3 (= 1 tr), (3 tr, ch 2, 4 tr) in next ch-sp, ch 1, (4 tr in next ch-sp, ch 1) 3 times, *(4 tr, ch 2, 4 tr) in next ch-sp, ch 1, (4 tr in next ch-sp, ch 1) 3 times, rep from * once more. Join with sl st in beg ch.

Rose Triangle

Beginning cluster: Ch 2, (insert hook into next st and pull up a loop) 3 times—4 loops on hook. Yarn around hook, pull yarn through all 4 loops on hook.
Cluster: (Insert hook into next st and pull up a loop) 4 times—5 loops on hook. Yarn around hook, pull yarn through all 4 loops on hook.

Make a magic ring (see page 74).
Rnd 1: Ch 1, dc 9 in ring; join to first dc with sl st.
Rnd 2: Ch 4, sk 2 dc, *1 sl st in next dc, ch 3, sk 2 dc; rep from * around—3 ch-spaces. Join with sl st in first ch.
Rnd 3: Ch 1, 1 dc in same st, (1 sl st, 3 tr, 1 sl st) in each ch-sp—3 petals. Join with sl st in beg ch.

Rnd 4: Ch 3, *sl st in center dc of petal, ch 3, 1 sl st in sl st between petals; rep from * around, sl st in first ch-sp to join—6 petals. Join with sl st in beg ch.

Rnd 5: Ch 1, (1 dc, 4 tr, 1 dc) in each ch-sp around, sl st in first ch to join.

Rnd 6: Ch 5, *1 sl st between next 2 petals, ch 4; rep from * around, sl st to beg ch-sp to join.

Rnd 7: Ch 1, (1 dc, 5 tr, 1 dc) in each ch-sp around, sl st to first dc to join.

Rnd 8: Join new color with sl st to the last dc of a petal, work 1 beg cluster in the same st, ch 3, 1 cluster in next dc, ch 3, 1 dc in center tr of next petal, ch 2, 1 tr between petals, ch 2, 1 dc in center of next tr petal, ch 3, *1 cluster in last dc of next petal, ch 3, 1 cluster in first dc of next petal, ch 3, 1 dc in center tr of next petal, ch 2, 1 tr between petals, ch 2, 1 dc in center of next tr petal, ch 3; rep from * around. Join with sl st in the top of the beg cluster.

Rnd 9: Join new color with sl st to a 3-ch sp between 2 clusters. Work (1 beg cluster, ch 6, 1 cluster) in the same sp, ch 3, (1 cluster, ch 2) in the next 3 ch-spaces, 1 cluster in the next ch-sp, ch 3, *(1 cluster, ch 6, 1 cluster) in the next ch-sp, ch 3, (1 cluster, ch 2) in the next 3 ch-spaces, 1 cluster in the following ch-sp, ch 3; rep from * once more. Join with sl st at the top of the beg cluster.

Rnd 10: Join new color with sl st to a 6-ch sp. (Ch 4 (= 1 dtr), 2 dtr, ch 1, 1 ttr, ch 1, 3 dtr) in the same sp, 4 tr in next ch-sp, (3 tr in next ch-sp) 3 times, 4 tr in next ch-sp, *(3 dtr, ch 1, 1 ttr, ch 1, 3 dtr) in next ch-sp, 4 tr in nex ch-sp, (3 tr in next ch-sp) 3 times, 4 tr in next ch-sp; rep from * once more. Join with sl st in third ch.

Circle

Make a magic ring (see page 74).

Rnd 1: Ch 5 (= 1 tr plus 2 ch), (1 tr, ch 2) 5 times around—6 ch-spaces. Join with sl st to top of ch 3.

Rnd 2: Join new color with sl st in a chain sp. Ch 3 (= 1 tr), 3 tr in first ch-sp, (4 tr in next ch-sp) around. Join with sl st to top of beg ch.

Rnd 3: Join new color with sl st in 3rd ch. Ch 1 (= 1 dc), 1 dc in same st, ch 3, sk 1, *1 dc in next tr, ch 3, sk 1* rep * to *, around. Join with sl st in first ch.

Rnd 4: Join new color with sl st in a ch-sp. Ch 5 (= 1 dc plus ch 4), *1 dc in next ch-sp, ch 4; rep from * around. Join with sl st in beg ch.

Rnd 5: Join with sl st in first ch, ch 1, (3 tr, 1 dc) in the same ch-sp, *(1 dc, 3 tr, 1 dc) in the following ch-sp; rep from * around—12 petals. Join with sl st in beg ch.

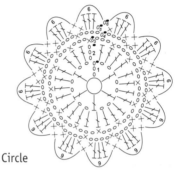

Circle

Rnd 6: Join a new color with sl st between 2 petals. Ch 7 (= 1 dc plus ch 6), *1 dc between the next 2 petals, ch 6; rep from * around. Join with sl st in the first ch.

Fasten off.

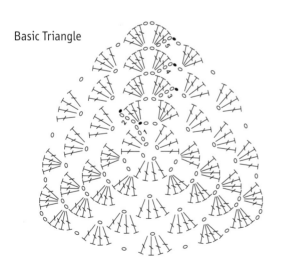

Basic Triangle

Rose Triangle

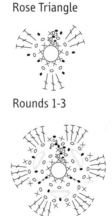

Rounds 1-3

Rounds 4 and 5

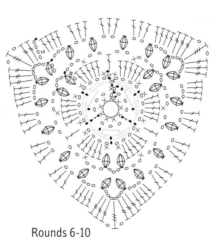

Rounds 6-10

Hexagon

Beg cluster: Ch 2, (insert hook into next st and draw up a loop) 3 times—4 loops on hook. Yarn around hook and draw through all loops on hook.
Cluster: (Insert hook into next st and draw up a loop) 4 times—5 loops on hook. Yarn around hook and draw through all loops on hook.

Make a magic ring (see page 74).
Rnd 1: Ch 3 (= 1 tr), 1 tr, ch 1, (2 tr, ch 1) 4 more times. Join with sl st in beg ch.
Rnd 2: Join new color with sl st in a ch-sp. Work 1 beg cluster, ch 1, 1 cluster in the same ch-sp, ch 2, *(1 cluster, ch 1, 1 cluster) in next ch-sp, ch 2; rep from * 4 more times. Join with sl st in the top of beg cluster.
Rnd 3: Join new color with sl st in a 2-ch sp. Work 1 beg cluster, ch 2, 1 cluster) in same ch-sp, ch 1, 2 tr between next 2

Hexagon Flower

Beg cluster: Ch 2, (yarn around hook, insert hook into next st and draw up a loop) 3 times—7 loops on hook. Yo and draw through all loops on hook.
Cluster: *Yarn around hook, insert hook into next st and draw up a loop) 4 times—9 loops on hook. Yo and draw through all loops on hook.

Make a magic ring (see page 74).
Rnd 1: Ch 3 (= 1 tr), 11 tr in ring. Join with sl st in beg ch.

Rnd 2: Join new color with sl st in first tr. Work beg cluster in same st, ch 2, *(1 cluster, ch 2) in next st; rep from * 10 more times. Join with sl st in the top of the beg cluster.
Rnd 3: Join new color with sl st in a ch-sp. (Ch 3 [= 1 tr], 1 tr, ch 2, 2 tr) in next ch-sp, 3 tr in next ch-sp, *(2 tr, ch 2, 2 tr) in next ch-sp, 3 tr in next ch-sp; rep from * around. Join with sl st in beg ch.
Rnd 4: Ch 1, (1 dc in each tr, 3 dc in each ch-sp) around. Join with sl st in beg ch.

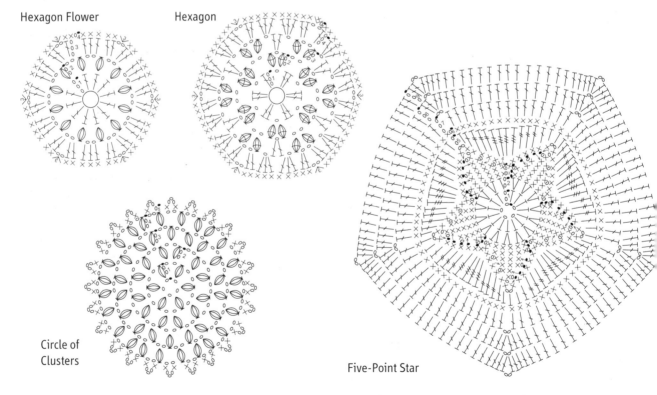

Hexagon Flower

Hexagon

Circle of Clusters

Five-Point Star

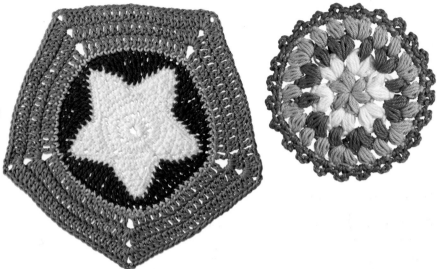

clusters, ch 1, *(1 cluster, ch 2, 1 cluster) in the next 2-ch sp, ch 1, 2 tr between next 2 clusters, ch 1; rep from * another 4 times, join with sl st in the top of beg cluster.

Rnd 4: Join new color with sl st in a 2-ch sp, (ch 3 [= 1 tr], 1 tr, ch 2, 2 tr) in same ch-sp, (3 tr in next ch-1 sp) twice, *(2 tr, ch 2, 2 tr) in next ch-sp, (3 tr in next ch-1 sp) twice; rep from * 4 more times. Join with sl st in beg ch.

Rnd 5: Join new color with sl st in a ch-sp, ch 1, 2 dc in same ch-sp, 1 dc in each tr around, working 3 dc in each corner ch-sp. Join with sl st in beg ch.

Five-Point Star

Ch 5, join with sl st in first ch to form a ring.

Rnd 1: Ch 2 (= 1 htr), 14 htr in ring. Join with sl st in beg ch.

Rnd 2: Work 2 htr in each htr around—30 sts. Join with sl st in beg ch.

Rnd 3: Work the star points back and forth as foll: *Ch 1, 1 dc in each of next 6 sts, ch 1, turn, 1 dc in each of next 5 sts, ch 1, turn, 1 dc in each of next 4 sts, ch 1, turn, 1 dc in each of next 3 sts, ch 1, turn, 1 dc in next each of 2 sts, ch 1, turn, 1 dc in next st, ch 1, turn. The WS is now facing you. Work 6 sl st (1 sl st in each row) along the side of the point. Sl st into the same st of Rnd 2 where the last dc was worked. Rep from * 4 more times—5 points.

Rnd 4: Ch 1, *Work 6 dc along side of point (1 dc in each row, working into 1 loop), (1 dc, ch 2, 1 dc) at point, 1 dc in the back loop of each of the following 6 sl st; rep from * 4 more times. Join with sl st in beg ch.

Rnd 5: Join new color with sl st in ch-sp at the top of one point. Ch 2 (= 1 htr), 1 htr in first dc; 1 tr in next st, 1 dtr in each of next 3 sts, 1 ttr in each of next 4 sts, 1 dtr in each of next 3 sts, 1 tr in next st, 1

htr in next st, *1 htr in ch-sp at top of next point, 1 htr in next st, 1 tr in next st, 1 dtr in each of next 3 sts, 1 ttr in each of next 4 sts, 1 tr in each of next 4 sts, 1 dtr in each of each of next 3 sts, 1 tr in next st, 1 htr in next st; rep from * 3 more times. Join with sl st in beg ch.

Rnd 6: Join new color with sl st. Ch 1, 1 dc in each st around, join with sl st in ch—75 sts.

Rnd 7: Join new color with sl st at the tip of a point. Ch 3 (= 1 tr), 1 tr in next 14 sts, ch 2, *1 tr in next 15 sts, ch 2; rep from * 3 more times. Join with sl st in top of beg ch.

Rnds 8 and 9: Ch 3 (=1 tr), *tr in each tr to next ch-sp, (2 tr, ch 2, 2 tr) in each ch-sp; rep from * 4 more times. Fasten off.

Circle of Clusters

Beg cluster: Ch 2, (yarn around hook, insert hook into next st and draw up a loop) 3 times—7 loops on hook. Yo and draw through all loops on hook.

Cluster: *(Yarn around hook, insert hook into next st and draw up a loop) 4 times—9 loops on hook. Yo and draw through all loops on hook.

Ch 5. Sl st to first ch to form a ring.

Rnd 1: Work beg cluster, ch 2, *1 cluster, ch 2; rep from * 4 more times. Join with sl st in the top of beg cluster.

Rnd 2: Join new color with sl st in a ch-sp, work (beg cluster, ch 2, 1 cluster) in same ch-sp, ch 2, *(1 cluster, ch 2, 1 cluster) in next ch-sp, ch 2; rep from * 4 more times. Join with sl st in top of beg cluster.

Rnd 3: Join new color with sl st in ch-sp between 2 pairs of clusters. Work (1 beg cluster, ch 2, 1 cluster) in same ch-sp, ch 2, 1 cluster in next ch-sp, ch 2, *(1 cluster, ch 2, 1 cluster) in next ch-sp, ch 2, 1 cluster in next ch-sp, ch 2; rep from * 4 more times. Join with sl st in top of beg cluster.

Rnd 4: Join new color with sl st in a ch-sp, work (1 beg cluster, ch 2, 1 cluster) in same ch-sp, ch 2, work (1 cluster, ch 2) in each of the next 2 ch-sp, ch 2, *(1 cluster, ch 2, 1 cluster) in next ch-sp, work (1 cluster ch 2) in each of the next 2 ch-sp; rep from * 4 more times. Join with sl st in top of beg cluster.

Rnd 5: Join new color with sl st in ch-sp, ch 4, 1 dc in same ch-sp, *(1 dc, ch 3, 1 dc) in next ch-sp; rep from * around. Join with sl st in first ch. Fasten off.

Simple Solid Triangle

Make a magic ring (see page 74).
Rnd 1: (4 tr in ring, ch 4) 3 times.
Rnds 2-4: Ch 3 (=1 tr), work 1 tr in each tr and (3 tr, ch 4, 3 tr) in each ch-sp around; join with sl st in beg ch.
Rnd 5: Ch 3 (= 1 tr), work 1 tr in each tr and (3 tr, ch 3, 3 tr) in each ch-sp. Join with sl st in beg ch.
Rnd 6: Join new color with sl st in the tr after a ch-sp, ch 1, work 1 dc in each tr and work (2 dc, ch 2, 2 dc) in each ch-sp around, join with sl st to beg ch.

Circle in Triangle

Ch 5, sl st to first ch to form a ring.
Rnd 1: Ch 3 (= 1 tr), 17 tr in ring; join with sl st in beg ch.
Rnd 2: Join new color with sl st between 2 tr, ch 3 (= 1 tr), 1 tr in same sp, 1 tr between next 2 tr, *2 tr between next 2 tr, 1 tr between next 2 tr; rep from * around—27 tr. Join with sl st in beg ch.
Rnd 3: Join new color with sl st in any tr, ch 3 (=1 tr), 1 tr in same st, ch 3, 2 tr in next st, ch 2, sk 1, 1 htr in next st, ch 2, sk 1 st, 1 dc in next st, ch 2, sk 1, 1 htr in next st, ch 2, sk 1, *2 tr in the next st, ch 3, 2 tr in next st, ch 2, sk 1, 1 htr in next st, ch 2, sk 1, dc in next st, ch 2, sk 1,

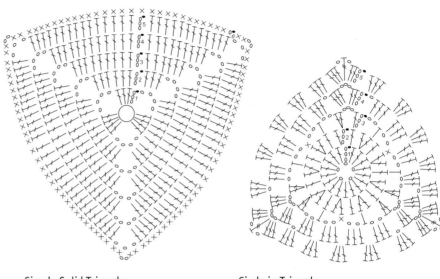

Simple Solid Triangle   Circle in Triangle

1 htr in next st, ch 2, sk 1; rep from * once more. Join with sl st in beg ch.
Rnd 4: Join new color in a 3-ch sp, ch 3 (= 1 tr) 2 tr, ch 3, 3 tr in same ch-sp, ch 1, 3 tr in each of the next 4 ch-spaces, ch 1, *(3 tr, ch 3, 3 tr) in each of the next 3 ch-spaces, ch 1; 3 tr in next 4 ch-spaces, ch 1, rep from * around, join with sl st in

top of beg ch.
Rnd 5: Join new color with sl st in a 3-ch sp, (ch 3 [= 1 tr], 2 tr, ch 1, 1 dtr, ch 1, 1 tr) in same ch-sp, 3 dc in each of the next 5 spaces between the groups of 3 tr, *(3 tr, ch 1, 1 dtr, ch 1, 3 tr) in each of the next 3 ch-spaces, 3 tr in each of the next 5 spaces between the groups of 3 tr; rep from * once more. Join with sl st in beg ch. Fasten off.

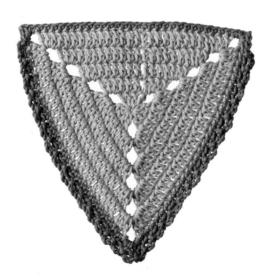

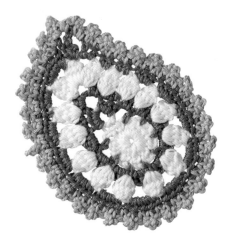

Paisley

Beg cluster: Ch 2, (insert hook into next st and draw up a loop) 3 times—4 loops on hook. Yo and draw through all loops on hook.
Cluster: *(Insert hook into next st and draw up a loop) 4 times—5 loops on hook. Yo and draw through all loops on hook.

Ch 4. Sl st to first ch to form a ring.
Rnd 1: Ch 2 (= 1 htr), 1 htr, ch 1, 1 htr, ch 6, sl st in 6th ch, 1 htr in the ring, ch 1, *2 htr, ch 1; rep from * 5 more times, sl st to beg ch to join.
Rnd 2: Join new color with sl st in the first ch-sp before the 6-ch sp, 1 htr, ch 1, (3 htr, ch 4, 3 htr) in the 6-ch sp, ch 1, 1 htr in the next ch-sp, ch 2, *1 dc in the next ch-sp, ch 2; rep from * 5 more times, sl st to join.
Rnd 3: Ch 1, 2 dc in next ch-sp, ch 1, sk 1 htr, 1 dc in the next 2 htr, ch 1, (2 dc, ch 4, 2 dc) in the 4-ch sp, ch 1, sk 1 htr, 1 dc in each of the next 2 htr, ch 1, *(2 dc, ch 1) in the next ch-sp; rep from * 7 more times. Join with sl st in beg ch.
Rnd 4: Join new color with sl st in a 4-ch sp, (ch 4, 1 cluster, ch 3, 1 cluster) in the

same ch-sp, ch 1, *1 cluster in the next ch-sp, ch 2; rep from * two more times, **1 cluster in the next ch-sp, ch 3; rep from ** 8 more times, ch 1, join with sl st in first ch.
Rnd 5. Join new color with sl st in the top of a middle cluster, *(ch 5, 1 ttr) in same st, ch 2, (1 tr, 1 htr) in the next ch-sp, *1 htr in next cluster, 1 htr in next ch-sp; rep from * once more, 1 htr in next cluster, 2 htr in next ch-sp, **1 htr in next cluster, 3 htr in next ch-sp; rep from ** two more times, ***1 htr in next cluster, 4 htr in next ch-sp; rep from *** once more, ****1 htr in next cluster, 3 htr in next ch-sp; rep from **** 5 more times, 1 tr in same ch-sp, ch 1. Join with sl st in 3rd ch.
Rnd 6: Join new color with sl st in a ch-sp to the right of a ttr, ch 1 (dc, picot = ch 3, 1 sl st in the first ch) in the same ch-sp, 2 dc in next ch-sp, picot, *1 dc in each of the next 2 sts, picot; rep from * around, 1 dc in second to last ch-sp, 1 dc in the last ch-sp, picot. Join with sl st in beg ch.

Simple Hexagon

Make a magic ring (see page 74).
Rnd 1: Ch 3 (=1 tr), work 11 tr in ring. Join with sl st in beg ch.
Rnd 2: Ch 3 (= 1 tr), 1 tr in same st, and then work 2 tr in each tr around. Join with sl st in beg ch.
Rnd 3: Ch 3 (=1 tr), 1 tr in each of next 2 tr, 5 tr in next tr, *1 tr in next 3 tr, 5 tr in next tr; rep from * 4 more times. Join with sl st in beg ch.
Rnd 4: Join new color with sl st in the center tr of a 5-tr group, ch 1, 2 dc in same st, 1 dc in each of next 7 tr, *3 dc in next st, 1 dc in each of next 7 sts; rep from * 4 more times. Join with sl st in beg ch.
Fasten off.

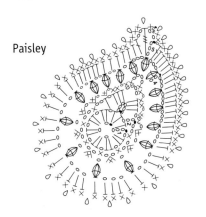

Paisley

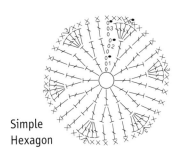

Simple Hexagon

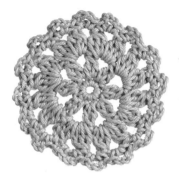

Rectangle

Rnd 1: Ch 16, turn, 1 tr in 5th ch from hook. 1 tr in each of next 2 ch, (ch 1, sk 1, 1 tr in each of next 3 ch) twice, ch 3. Join with sl st in beg ch.
Rnd 2: Join new color with sl st in 5-ch sp. Ch 3 (= 1 tr), work (2 tr, ch 3, 3 tr, ch 3, 3 tr) in the same ch-sp, ch 1, 3 tr in the next ch-sp, ch 1, 3 tr in next ch-sp, ch 1, (3 tr, ch 3, 3 tr, ch 3, 3 tr) in the next 5-ch sp, (ch 1, 3 tr in next ch-sp) twice, ch 1. Join with sl st in beg ch.
Rnd 3: Join new color in the first 1-ch sp after a corner. Ch 3 (= 1 tr), work 2 tr in same ch-sp, ch 1, (3 tr in next ch-sp, ch 1) twice, *([3 tr, ch 3, 3 tr] in next 3-ch sp, ch 1) twice*, (3 tr in next ch-sp, ch 1) 3 times, rep from * to * once more. Join with sl st in beg ch.

Flower

Make a magic ring (see page 74).
Rnd 1: Ch 2 (= 1 htr), work 11 htr in ring. Join with sl st in beg ch.
Rnd 2: Join new color with sl st in htr, ch 2 (= 1 htr), 1 htr in same st, 2 htr in each htr round. Join with sl st in beg ch.
Rnd 3: Join new color with sl st in htr, ch 1, 1 sc in each of next 2 htr, ch 3, *1 dc in each of next 3 htr, ch 3; rep from * 6 more times. Join with sl st in beg ch.
Rnd 4: Ch 1, 1 dc in next dc, 6 tr in next ch-sp, *1 dc in the center of the next group of 3 dc, 6 tr in next ch-sp; rep from * 6 more times. Join with sl st in beg ch.

Monochrome Circle

Beg 2-st Cluster: Ch 2, yo, insert hook into next st and draw up loop—2 loops on hook, yo, draw yarn through both loops on hook.
2-st Cluster: (Yarn around hook, insert hook into next st and draw up loop) twice—3 loops on hook, yarn around hook, draw yarn through all loops on hook.
Beg 3-st Cluster: Ch 2, (yarn around hook, insert hook into next st and draw up loop) twice—3 loops on hook, yarn around hook, draw yarn through all loops on hook.
3-st Cluster: (Yarn around hook, insert hook into next st and draw up loop) 3 times—4 loops on hook, yarn around hook, draw yarn through all loops on hook.

Make a magic ring (see page 74).
Rnd 1: Ch 1, 8 dc in ring; join with sl st in first dc.
Rnd 2: Beg 2-st cluster, ch 3, *2-st cluster, ch 3 in the next dc; rep from * around; join with sl st in the top of the beg cluster.
Rnd 3: Sl st in the next ch-sp, (beg 3-st cluster, ch 3, 3-st cluster, ch 3) in the same ch-sp, *(3-st cluster, ch 3, 3-st cluster, ch 3) in the next ch-sp; rep 6 more times. Join with sl st in the top of the beg cluster.
Rnd 4: Ch 1 (1 dc, ch 3,1 dc) in each ch-sp around; join with sl st in first ch.

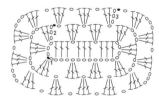

Rectangle

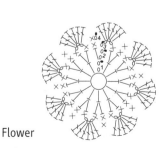

Flower

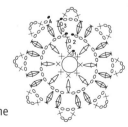

Monochrome Circle

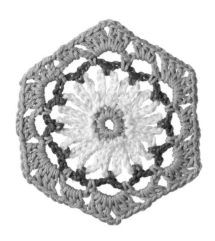  

Mesh Flower

Ch 5, sl st in first ch to form a ring.
Rnd 1: Ch 1, 12 dc in ring; join with sl st in first dc.
Rnd 2: Join new color with sl st in a dc, ch 10, sl st in the same st, *1 sl st in next st, ch 10, 1 sl st in the same st; rep from * around—12 ch-spaces. Join with sl st in beg ch.
Rnd 3: Join new color with sl st in a ch-sp, ch 5, *1 dc in next ch-sp, ch 4; rep from * around. Join with sl st in beg ch.
Rnd 4: Join new color with sl st in a ch-sp, ch 6, *1 dc in next ch-sp, ch 5; rep from * around. Join with sl st in beg ch.
Rnd 5: Sl st in next ch-sp, ch 3 (= 1 tr), (2 tr, ch 2, 3 tr) in same ch-sp, ch 1, 3 htr in next ch-sp, ch 1, *(3 tr, ch 2, 3 tr) in next ch-sp, ch 1, 3 htr in next ch-sp, ch 1; rep from * 4 more times. Join with sl st in beg ch.

Small Star

Make a magic ring (see page 74).
Rnd 1: Ch 1, 12 dc in ring; join with sl st in first dc.
Rnd 2: Ch 2 (= 1 htr), 1 htr in same st, then work 2 htr in each dc around—24 htr. Join with sl st in beg ch.
Rnd 3: Join new color with sl st in a htr. Ch 3 (= 1 tr), 1 tr in each of next 3 htr, ch 4, *1 tr in each of next 4 htr, ch 4; rep from * 4 more times. Join with sl st in beg ch.
Rnd 4: Sl st in next tr, *1 dc between the two center tr in the 4-tr group, ch 1 (4 tr, ch 3, 4 tr) in next ch-sp, ch 1; rep from * 5 more time; join with sl st in first dc.

Flower in Concentric Circles

Beg cluster: Ch 2, (yarn around hook, insert hook into next st and draw up a loop, yarn around hook pull through 2 loops on hook) twice—3 loops on hook. Yarn around hook and draw through all loops on hook.
Cluster: *(Yarn around hook, insert hook into next st and draw up a loop, yarn around hook, pull through 2 loops on hook) 3 times—4 loops on hook. Yarn around hook and draw through all loops on hook.

Make a magic ring (see page 74).
Rnd 1: Ch 1, 6 dc in ring, join with sl st in beg ch.
Rnd 2: Join new color to a dc, (ch 1, beg cluster, ch 4) in the same st, (1 cluster, ch 4) in each dc around—6 clusters. Join with sl st in the top of the beg cluster.

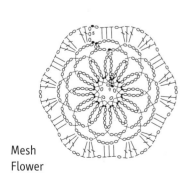 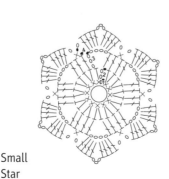 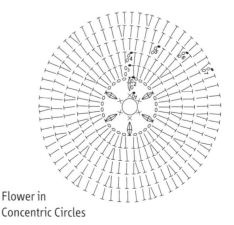

Mesh
Flower

Small
Star

Flower in
Concentric Circles

Rnd 3: Join new color with sl st in a ch-sp. Ch 2 (= 1 htr), 6 htr in same ch-sp, work 7 htr in each ch-sp around. Join with sl st in beg ch.

Rnd 4: Join new color with sl st in 1 htr, ch 2 (= 1 htr), 1 htr in same st, 1 htr in each of next 5 sts, *2 htr in next st, 1 htr in each of next 5 sts; rep from * around. Join with sl st in beg ch.

Rnd 5: Join new color with sl st in a htr that is in the center of the 5 tr between increases on the previous rnd. Ch 2 (= 1 htr), 1 htr in same st, 1 htr in each of the next 6 htr, *2 htr in next st, 1 htr in each of next 6 sts; rep from * around. Join with sl st in beg ch.

Rnd 6: Join new color with sl st in a htr (as on Rnd 5). Ch 2 (= 1 htr), 1 htr in same st, 1 htr in each of the next 7 htr, *2 htr in next st, 1 htr in each of next 7 sts; rep from * around. Join with sl st in 2nd beg ch. Join with sl st in beg ch.

Rnd 7: Join new color with sl st in a htr (as on Rnd 5). Ch 2 (= 1 htr), 1 htr in same st, 1 htr in each of the next 8 htr, *2 htr in next st, 1 htr in each of next 8 sts; rep from * around. Join with sl st in beg ch.

Pentagon with Flower

Make a magic ring (see page 74).
Rnd 1: Ch 1, 5 dc in ring, join with sl st in beg ch.
Rnd 2: Join new color with sl st in a dc, (ch 3, 3 tr, ch 3, sl st) in same dc (1 petal completed), *(sl st, ch 3, 3 tr, ch 3, sl st) in next dc (next petal completed); rep from * 3 more times. Join with sl st in beg ch.
Rnd 3: Join new color with sl st behind petal in back loop of the center tr, ch 4, *sl st behind petal in back loop of the center tr, ch 3; rep from * 3 more times, join with sl st in first ch-sp.
Rnd 4: Ch 2 (= 1 htr), 3 htr in same ch-sp, ch 2, *4 htr in next ch-sp, ch 2; rep from * 3 more times. Join with sl st in beg ch.

Rnd 5: Join new color with sl st in ch-sp. Ch 3 (= 1 tr), 7 tr in same ch-sp, 1 dc in center of next 4-htr group, *8 tr in next ch-sp, 1 dc in center of next 4-htr group; rep from* 3 more times. Join with sl st in beg ch.
Rnd 6: Join new color with sl st in dc. Ch 3 (= 1 tr), 8 tr in same dc, 1 dc each in 4th and 5th tr of the next petal, *9 tr in next dc, 1 dc each in 4th and 5th tr of the next petal; rep from * 3 more times. Join with sl st in beg ch.

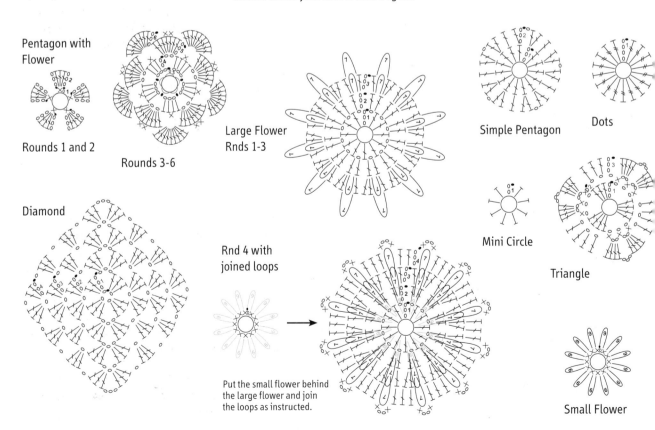

Pentagon with Flower

Rounds 1 and 2

Rounds 3-6

Large Flower
Rnds 1-3

Simple Pentagon

Dots

Mini Circle

Triangle

Diamond

Rnd 4 with joined loops

Put the small flower behind the large flower and join the loops as instructed.

Small Flower

Radiant Blossom

Note: The Radiant Blossom is worked in two parts, with a small flower and a large flower, which are joined together to make up a 12-petaled flower.

Small Flower

Make a magic ring (see page 74).
Rnd 1: Ch 1, *1 dc in ring, ch 9; rep from * 11 more times; join with sl st in first dc. Fasten off.

Large Flower

Make a magic ring (see page 74).
Rnd 1: With new color, ch 4 (= 1 tr + ch 1), *1 tr in ring, ch 1; rep from * 10 more times; join with sl st in 3rd ch.
Rnd 2: With new color, ch 10 (= 1 tr + ch 7), 1 tr in ch-sp, *(1 tr, ch 7, 1 tr) in next ch-sp; rep from * 10 more times; join with sl st.
Rnd 3: Ch 3 (= 1 tr), 1 tr in the same tr of previous rnd, ch 7, 1 tr in next tr, *2 tr next tr, ch 7, 1 tr in next tr; rep from * 10 more times. Join with sl st in beg ch. Place the small flower behind the center of the large flower. Insert the crochet hook into a 1-ch sp in the first rnd of the large flower, and pull a 9-ch loop from the small flower to the front. *Leave the hook in the loop and draw the 7-ch loop from Rnd 2 of the larger flower to the front, then draw the 7-ch loop from Rnd 3 of the large flower to the front. Repeat to join the loops all the way around—12 loops total.

Rnd 4: With new color, ch 3 (= 1 tr), *1 tr in each tr from previous rnd, working (1 dc, ch 2, 1 dc) in the 7-ch loop; rep from * 11 more times. Join with sl st in beg ch.

Mini Circle

Make a magic ring (see page 74).
Rnd 1: Ch 2 (= 1 htr), work 8 htr in ring. Join with sl st in beg ch.

Diamond

Ch 4, sl st in first ch to form a ring.
Rnd 1: Ch 3 (= 1 tr), 2 tr, ch 1, 3 tr, ch 3, 3 tr, ch 1, 3 tr, ch 3 in the ring. Join with sl st in beg ch.
Rnd 2: Join new color with sl st to 1-ch sp, ch 3 (= 1 tr), (2 tr, ch 1, 3 tr) in same ch-sp, ch 1, (3 tr, ch 3, 3 tr) in next 3-ch sp, ch 1, (3 tr, ch 1, 3 tr) in next 1-ch sp, ch 1, (3 tr, ch 3, 3 tr) in next 3-ch sp, ch 1. Join with sl st in beg ch.
Rnd 3: Join new color with sl st in a 1-ch sp on a corner of the previous rnd, ch 3 (= 1 tr), (2 tr, ch 1, 3 tr) in same ch-sp, ch 1, 3 tr in next 1-ch sp, ch 1, (3 tr, ch 3, 3 tr) in next 3-ch sp, ch 1, 3 tr in next 1-ch sp, ch 1, (3 tr, ch 1, 3 tr) in next ch-sp, ch 1, 3 tr in next 1-ch sp, ch 1, (3 tr, ch 3, 3 tr) in next 3-ch sp, ch 1, 3 tr in next 1-ch sp, ch 1. Join with sl st in beg ch.
Rnd 4: Join new color with sl st in 1-ch sp on a corner of the previous rnd, ch 3 (= 1 tr), (2 tr, ch 1, 3 tr) in same ch-sp, (ch 1, 3 tr in next 1-ch sp) twice, ch 1, (3 tr, ch 3, 3 tr) in next 3-ch sp, (ch 1, 3 tr in next 1-ch sp) twice, ch 1, (3 tr, ch 1, 3 tr in

same ch-sp, (ch 1, 3 tr in next 1-ch sp) twice, ch 1, (3 tr, ch 3, 3 tr) in next 3-ch sp, (ch 1, 3 tr in next 1-ch sp) twice, ch 1. Join with sl st to top of beg ch.

Simple Pentagon

Make a magic ring (see page 74).
Rnd 1: Ch 3 (= 1 tr), 14 tr in ring; sl st to join.
Rnd 2: With new color, ch 3 (= 1 tr), 1 tr in same tr, 1 tr in next tr, 2 tr in next tr, ch 1, *2 tr in next tr, 1 tr in next tr, 2 tr in next tr, ch 1; rep from * 3 more times. Join with sl st in beg ch.

Dots (Joining Circles)

Make a magic ring (see page 74).
Rnd 1: Ch 4 (= 1 tr), 17 tr in ring. Join with sl st in beg ch.

Triangle

Make a magic ring (see page 74).
Rnd 1: Ch 3 (= 1 tr), 3 tr in ring, ch 3, *4 tr in ring, ch 3; rep from * once more.
Rnd 2: Join new color, ch 1, *(1 dc, ch 2, 1 dc, ch 2, 1 dc) in ch-sp, ch 3, skip 4 tr, rep from * 2 more times; join with sl st in first dc. Join with sl st in beg ch.
Rnd 3: Join new color, ch 3 (= 1 tr), 3 tr in same 3-ch sp, 4 tr in next 2-ch sp, ch 3, 4 tr in next 2-ch sp, *4 tr in 3-ch sp, 4 tr in next 2-ch sp, ch 3, 4 tr in next 2-ch sp; rep from * once more. Join with sl st in beg ch.

Propeller

Ch 5, sl st in first ch to form a ring.
Rnd 1: Ch 5 (= 1 tr plus ch 2), 2 tr in the ring, *1 tr, ch 2, 2 tr in the ring; rep from * 4 more times, join with sl st in 3rd ch.
Rnd 2: Ch 1, *3 dc in ch-sp of previous rnd, sk 1 tr, 1 dc in each of next 2 tr; rep from * 5 more times; join with sl st in first dc.
Rnd 3: Ch 8 (= 1 tr plus ch 5), skip 2 dc of previous rnd, 1 tr in each of next 2 dc, *1 tr, ch 5, skip 2 dc of previous rnd, 1 tr in each of next 2 dc; rep from * 4 more times; join with sl st in 3rd ch.
Rnd 4: With new color, ch 1, * work 3 elongated tr in the next 2-ch sp of Rnd 1, dc in each of next 3 tr of previous rnd; rep from * 5 more times; join with sl st in beg ch.
Rnd 5: Ch 3 (= 1 tr), 1 tr in each of next 2 "long" tr, 1 tr in next dc, (1 tr, ch 2, 1 tr) in next dc, 1 tr in next st, *1 tr in each of next 3 "long" tr, 1 tr in next dc, (1 tr, ch 2, 1 tr) in next dc, 1 tr in next st; rep from * 4 more times and join with sl st in 3rd ch.

Star

Extended Treble Crochet (etr): Yarn around hook, insert the hook into the next st of the previous row and draw up the yarn, yarn around hook, draw yarn through one loop on hook, complete st as for a normal tr.

Note: **Work each subsequent etr in the base of the previous etr.**

Make a magic ring (see page 74).
Rnd 1: Ch 3 (= 1 tr), 17 tr in ring.
Rnd 2: Join new color to tr in previous rnd. Ch 3 (=1 etr), 3 etr, ch 5, work 1 etr in each of the 4 previous etr, sk 2 tr, * 4 etr, ch 5, work 1 etr in each of the 4 previous etr, sk 2 tr; rep from * 4 more times.
Rnd 3: Join new color in a 5-ch sp, ch 1, *3 dc, ch 2, 3 dc in 5-ch sp, 1 dc in each of next 3 tr, dc2tog in next tr and next etr, 1 dc in each of foll 3 etr; rep from * 5 more times, join with sl st in first dc. Fasten off.

8 Corners (Octagon)

Long Back Post Stitch: Yarn around hook 4 times, insert hook around the post of specified stitch (see page 76) several rows below and draw up a loop, yo and draw yarn through 2 loops at a time until 1 loop rem on hook.

Make a magic ring (see page 74).
Rnd 1: Ch 3 (= 1 tr), 15 tr in ring. Join with sl st in 3rd ch.
Rnd 2: With new color, ch 3 (= 1 tr), 1 tr in tr of previous rnd, 2 tr in next tr, ch 1, * 2 tr in next tr, 2 tr in next tr, ch 1; rep from * 6 more times. Join with sl st.
Rnd 3: With new color, ch 3 (= 1 tr), 1 tr in 1st tr of previous rnd, 1 tr in each of next 2 tr, 2 tr in next tr, ch 1, * 2 tr in next tr, 1 tr in each of next 2 tr, 2 tr in next tr, ch 1; rep from * 6 more times. Join with sl st in beg ch.
Rnd 4: With new color, ch 3 (= 1 tr), 1 tr in each of next 2 tr, work long back post stitch in 1st tr of Rnd 1, 1 tr in each of next 3 tr, ch 1, *1 tr in each of next 3 tr, work long back post stitch in next tr of Rnd 1, 1 tr in each of next 3 tr, ch 1; rep

Four Corners

Make a magic ring (see page 74).
Rnd 1: Ch 3 (= 1 tr), work 15 tr in ring; join with sl st in beg ch.
Rnd 2: Join new color with sl st to tr, ch 4 (counts as 1 tr and ch 1), 1 tr in same tr, 2 tr in next tr, 1 tr, 2 tr in next tr, * (1 tr, ch 1, 1 tr) in next tr, 2 tr in next tr, 1 tr, 2 tr in next tr, rep from * 2 more times. Join with sl st in beg ch.

Propeller

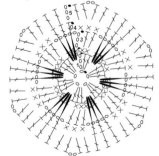

Four Corners

Star

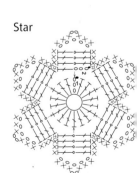

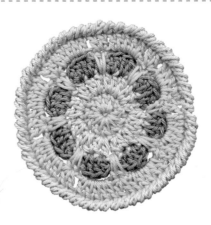

from * 6 more times, with with long back post stitch being worked into every other stitch of Rnd 1. Join with sl st in beg ch.

5 Corners (Pentagon)

Make a magic ring (see page 74).
Rnd 1: Ch 3 (= 1 tr), 9 tr in ring; join with sl st in 3rd ch.
Rnd 2: Ch 3 (= 1 tr), 1 tr in 1st tr of previous rnd, *2 tr in each tr around; join with sl st in 3rd ch.
Rnd 3: Ch 3 (= 1 tr), tr in 1st tr of previous rnd, 1 tr in each of next 2 tr, 2 tr in next tr, *1 tr in each of next 2 tr, 2 tr in next tr; rep from * 3 more times. Join with sl st in beg ch.
Rnd 4: Ch 3 (= 1 tr), 1 tr in each of next

2 tr, work long back post stitch in 1st tr of Rnd 1, 1 tr in each of next 3 tr, *1 tr in each of next 3 tr, 1 long back post tr in next tr of Rnd 1, 1 tr in each of next 3 tr; rep from * 4 more times, with long back post stitch being worked into every other stitch of Rnd 1. Join with sl st in beg ch.

4 Corners (Square)

Make a magic ring (see page 74).
Rnd 1: Ch 3 (= 1 tr), 15 tr in ring. Join with sl st in 3rd ch.
Rnd 2: Ch 3 (= 1 tr), 1 tr in first tr of previous rnd, 1 tr in each of next 2 tr, 2 tr in next tr, ch 1, *2 tr in next tr of previous rnd, 1 tr in each of next 2 tr, 2 tr in next tr, ch 1; rep from * 2 more times. Join with sl st in beg ch.

3 Corners (Triangle)

Make a magic ring (see page 74).
Rnd 1: Ch 3 (= 1 tr), 5 tr in ring, ch 1, *6

tr in ring, ch 1; rep from * once more. Join with sl st in beg ch.

Flower in Circle

Note: When working the color change at the beg of Rnd 4, do not work a beg ch. Instead, work the first stitch until 1 loop rem on hook. Finish the stitch with the new color and work the rest of the stitches normally.

Make a magic ring (see page 74).
Rnd 1: Ch 3 (= 1 tr), 11 tr in ring. Join with sl st in 3rd ch.
Rnd 2: With new color, ch 3 (= 1 tr), tr in same st, work 2 tr in each tr around. Join with sl st in 3rd ch.
Rnd 3: In tr of the previous rnd, *1 dc, 2 tr in each of the next 2 tr; rep from * 7 more times around; join with sl st in the first dc.
Rnd 4: Join new color to a dc at the beg of previous rnd, *1 elongated htr between 2 tr on Rnd 2, ch 4, 1 elongated htr between 3rd and 4th tr in Rnd 2; rep from * 7 more times. Join with sl st in first st of new color.
Rnd 5: Ch 3 (= 1 tr), 1 tr in next 4 ch-sp, skip next elongated htr, 2 tr in next elongated htr, *5 tr in next 4-ch sp, skip next elongated htr, 2 tr in next elongated htr; rep from * 6 more times. Join with sl st in beg ch.
Rnd 6: With new color, ch 1, dc in each tr around. Join with sl st in beg ch.

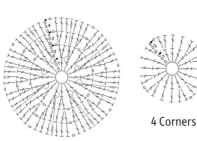

4 Corners

8 Corners

3 Corners

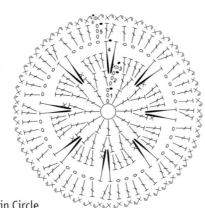

5 Corners

Flower in Circle

New Shapes, New Projects

In this chapter, the beauty of "granny" motifs becomes evident as they are combined together into enchanting projects to crochet. There's something for every skill level, from easy to advanced, but every project is beautiful. The fabulous seat cushions are unbelievably practical and the placemats make gossiping over coffee more fun than ever before. The crochet accessories are all so eye-catching that you will be amazed when you see the finished results.

Pretty Baskets

chic storage for odds and ends

EASY

FINISHED MEASUREMENTS
Diameter approx.
12 (14, 16) cm /
4¾ (5½, 6¼) in

Height approx.
9 cm / 3½ in

YARN
CYCA #2, Schachen-mayr Original Cata-nia or equivalent
(125 m/ 137 yd/ 50 g;
100% cotton).

YARN AMOUNTS
Pearl 255, approx.
100 g

Pale Green 262,
Cream 130, Raffia
257, Rose 246, and
Hyacinth 240,
approx. 50 g each

HOOKS
3 mm and 5 mm /
U.S. sizes C-2/D-3
and H-8

NOTIONS
Tapestry needle

GAUGE
20 dc and 24 rows
with smaller hook =
10 x 10 cm / 4 x 4 in

Instructions

With smaller hook, make 18 Monochrome Circles (see page 14): 7 with Pearl, 6 with Rose, and 5 with Cream.

Large Basket

With larger hook and one strand each of Green and Pearl held together, make a magic ring (see page 74).

Rnd 1: Ch 2 (= 1 hdc), 11 htr in ring, join rnd with sl st in 2nd ch.

Rnd 2: Ch 3 (= 1 tr in this and all foll rnds), work 2 tr in each htr around, join with sl st in 3rd ch.

Rnd 3: Ch 3, 2 tr in next tr, *1 tr in next tr, 2 tr in next tr; rep from * around, join with sl st in 3rd ch.

Rnd 4: Ch 3, 1 tr in next tr, 2 tr in next tr, *1 tr in each of next 2 tr, 2 tr in next tr; rep from * around, join with sl st in 3rd ch.

Rnd 5: Ch 3, 1 tr in each of next 2 tr, 2 tr in next tr, *1 tr in each of next 3 tr, 2 tr in next tr; rep from * around, join with sl st in 3rd ch.

Rnd 6: Ch 3, 1 tr in each of next 3 tr, 2 tr in next dc, *1 tr in each of next 4 tr, 2 tr in next tr; rep from * around, join with sl st in 3rd ch.

Rnds 7-14: Ch 3, 1 tr in each tr around, join with sl st in 3rd ch.

Medium Basket

With larger hook and one strand each of Hya-cinth and Rose held together, make a magic ring (see page 74).

Rnds 1-5: Work as for Large Basket.

Rnds 6-11: Ch 3, 1 tr in each tr around, join with sl st in 3rd ch.

Small Basket

With larger hook and one strand each of Raffia and Cream held together, make a magic ring (see page 74).

Rnds 1-4: Work as for Large Basket.

Rnds 5-11: Ch 3, 1 tr in each tr around, join with sl st in 3rd ch.

Finishing

Using the photo as a guide, sew the Circles so that they are evenly spaced around each basket.

Warm Baby Blanket
in sweet berry colors

EASY

FINISHED
MEASUREMENTS
Diameter approx.
110 x 110 cm / 43½ x
43½ in

YARN
Shown: CYCA #4,
Schachenmayr SMC
Micro Grande or
equivalent (199 m/
218 yd/ 100 g; 100%
microfiber).

YARN AMOUNTS
Apricot 135, Orchid
148, Azalea 137,
Plum 147, and
Natural 102, 200 g
each

SUBSTITUTION
Schachenmayr
Select Violena (95 m
/ 106 yd / 50 g).

HOOK
4 mm / U.S. size G-6

NOTIONS
Tapestry needle

GAUGE
16 dc and 17 rows =
10 x 10 cm / 4 x 4 in

Instructions

Make 127 Simple Hexagons (see page 13), working up to, and including, Rnd 3: 34 in Apricot (1), 30 in Plum (2), 30 in Azalea (3), and 33 in Orchid (4).
Crochet the Hexagons together, following the schematic (see page 77). Join vertical strips first, then horizontal seams. Work horizontal seams across the entire strip, working 1 dc at each join between motifs.

Finishing

Arrange the motifs as shown in the schematic. Join the motifs with crochet (see page 77): With Natural, sl st in the center of a 5-tr group at a corner, ch 1, then work 1 dc in each tr, and 3 dc in the center st of each 5-tr group at the corners. After all of the motifs are joined, work around the entire blanket for a border. Begin at a tr next to a seam and work tr around, working a decrease at each seam between motifs as foll: (yarn over, insert hook into next st and draw up a loop) twice, yarn around hook, draw yarn through all loops on hook.

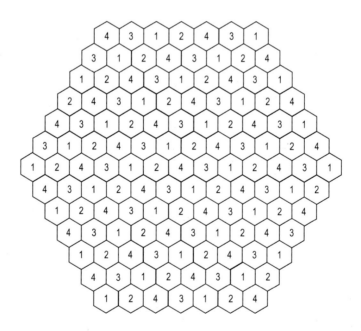

Cute Baby Beanie
pretty and fluffy

INTERMEDIATE

SIZE
Newborn to 6 months

FINISHED MEASUREMENTS
Head circumference approx. 40 cm / 15¾ in

YARN
CYCA #1, Schachenmayr Nomotta Baby Wool or equivalent and Baby Wool Color (85 m/ 93 yd/ 25 g; 100% merino).

YARN AMOUNTS
PINK HAT
Natural 02, 25 g and Pastel Pink 182, 50 g
BLUE HAT
Natural 02 and Navy 51, 25 g each; Light Blue 52, 50 g

HOOK
3 mm / U.S. size C-2/D-3

NOTIONS
Tapestry needle

GAUGE
28 dc and 36 rows = 10 x 10 cm / 4 x 4 in

Instructions

For Pink Hat

Make 4 Rose Triangles (see page 8), working Rnds 1-7 with Natural, Rnd 8 with Pastel Pink, Rnd 9 with Natural, and Rnd 10 with Pastel Pink.

For Blue Hat

Make 2 Circle in Triangle motifs (see page 12), working Rnd 1 in Navy, Rnd 2 in Light Blue, Rnd 3 in Navy, Rnd 4 in Natural, and Rnd 5 in Navy. Make 2 Circle in Triangle motifs (see page 12), working Rnd 1 in Light Blue, Rnd 2 in Navy, Rnd 3 in Light Blue, Rnd 4 in Natural, and Rnd 5 in Light Blue.

Following the schematic, join the Triangles in Natural for the pink hat and in Light Blue for the blue hat.

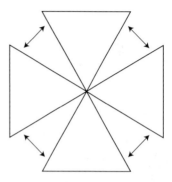

Finishing

Rnd 1: Join Pastel Pink for pink hat and Light Blue for blue hat with sl st to an edge stitch. Ch 3 (= 1 tr in this and foll rnds), 1 tr in each edge stitch around; join with sl st in 3rd ch.
Rnds 2-4: Ch 3, 1 tr in each tr around, working tr2tog in every 5th and 6th st; join with sl st in 3rd ch.
Rnds 5-8: Ch 3, 1 tr in each tr around, join with sl st in 3rd ch.
Rnds 9-11: Ch 2, 1 htr in each st around, join with sl st in 2rd ch.
Fasten off.

Combining the colors in different ways in this motif can be extremely effective.

Cozy Floor Cushion
chic and eye-catching

INTERMEDIATE

FINISHED MEASUREMENTS
Approx. 65 x 65 cm / 25½ x 25½ in

YARN
Shown: CYCA #4, Schachenmayr SMC Micro Grande or equivalent (199 m/ 218 yd/ 100 g).

YARN AMOUNTS
Blue 152, 200 g

Azalea 137, Kiwi 172, and White 101, 100 g each

SUBSTITUTION
Schachenmayr Select Violena (95 m / 106 yd / 50 g).

HOOK
4 mm / U.S. size G-6

NOTIONS
1 pillow form approx. 65 x 65 cm / 25½ x 25½ in; 3 pieces of linen fabric: 70 x 70 cm / 27½ x 27½ in, 60 x 70 cm / 23½ x 27½ in, and 34 x 70 cm / 13½ x 27½ in; sewing machine; sewing thread in natural and light blue

GAUGE
16 dc and 17 rows = 10 x 10 cm / 4 x 4 in

Instructions

Make 1 Mesh Flower (see page 15) in the following colors: Work Rnd 1 in Kiwi, Rnd 2 in White, Rnd 3 in Azalea, and Rnds 4-5 in Blue.

Work all 38 motifs the same way, joining them together as you crochet Rnd 5 (see page 77). Alternate between 1 row with 5 motifs and 1 row with 6 motifs, offsetting the motifs as shown in the photo. You will have 4 rows with 5 motifs and 3 rows with 6 motifs.

Lay the crochet piece on top of the 70 x 70 cm / 27½ x 27½ in piece of linen fabric, and pin in place at the joins between motifs and around the edge, leaving a 1 cm / ½ in seam allowance. With blue thread, tack the motifs to the fabric with hand stitches. Fold down a 2-cm / ¾ in hem on the long edge of the 60 x 70 cm / 23½ x 27½ in, and 34 x 70 cm / 13½ x 27½ in pieces of linen and stitch in place by machine.

Finishing

Place the piece of linen with crochet motifs attached crochet side up. Place the other two pieces of linen right side down with the hemmed edges overlapping to form the opening. Pin around edges and sew. Turn the pillow right side out and insert the pillow form.

Sweet Clutch
for small essentials

EASY

FINISHED MEASUREMENTS
Approx. 20 x 14 cm /
8 x 5½ in

YARN
CYCA #2, Schachenmayr Original Catania or equivalent (125 m/ 137 yd/ 50 g; 100% cotton).

YARN AMOUNTS
Light Blue 173, 100 g
Small amounts of Stone 242, Silver 172, and Sun 208

HOOK
3 mm / U.S. size C-2/D-3

NOTIONS
Satin fabric in gold (36 x 42 cm / 14 x 16½ in), 2 metal snaps (1.5 cm / ½ in), sewing needle, light blue sewing thread, tapestry needle

GAUGE
20 dc and 24 rows =
10 x 10 cm / 4 x 4 in

Instructions

Flower
Make 1 Flower (see page 14), working Rnd 1 in Sun, Rnd 2 in Silver, and Rnds 3-4 in Stone.

Purse
The purse is worked back and forth in rows. With Blue, ch 45.
Row 1: Ch 1, dc in 2nd ch from hook and in each ch across—45 dc. Turn.
Row 2: Ch 1, dc in each dc across, turn.
Repeat Row 2 until piece measures 35 cm / 13¾ in.
Weave in ends.
Dampen piece and dry flat.

Lining
Fold the fabric in half and sew all around the edges with a 1 cm / 3/8 in seam allowance, leaving a 5 cm / 2 in opening to turn the piece right side out. Turn and hand-stitch the opening closed.

Press the satin fabric with a cool iron or under a pressing cloth. Attach the lining to the crochet fabric and sew by hand around the edges. Fold the bottom of the bag up approx. 14 cm / 5½ in from the bottom and sew the sides together with Light Blue yarn.

Sew one half of each snap onto the flap approx. 4 cm / 1¾ in from the side and 1 cm / 3/8 in from the bottom edge of the flap. Sew the other side of each snap onto the bag, making sure they are aligned to close properly.

Finishing

Sew the Flower to the purse with Stone yarn and tapestry needle, using the photo as a guide.

My Tip for You

If you don't want a satin lining, you can instead line the purse in felt of a matching color. Cut the felt about the same size as the crocheted purse before sewing the seams, adding about 1 cm / 3/8 in seam allowance. Stitch the lining to the purse by hand.

Colorful Blanket
bright and decorative

EXPERIENCED

FINISHED MEASUREMENTS
Approx. 160 x 160 cm / 63 x 63 in

YARN
Shown: CYCA #4, Schachenmayr SMC Micro Grande or equivalent (199 m / 218 yd / 100 g; 100% microfiber).

YARN AMOUNTS
Capri 168, 900 g
Orchid 148, 500 g
Kiwi 172, 400 g
White 101, 300 g
Sun 121, 200 g

SUBSTITUTION
Schachenmayr Select Violena (95 m/ 106 yd/ 50 g).

HOOK
4 mm / U.S. size G-6

NOTIONS
Tapestry needle

GAUGE
16 sc and 17 rows = 10 x 10 cm / 4 x 4 in

Instructions

Make 203 Circles (see page 9), working Rnd 1 in Sun, Rnd 2 in Orchid, Rnd 3 in White and Rnds 4 & 5 in Capri.
On the first Circle, work Rnd 6 with Kiwi. Work the remaining motifs, joining them together as you crochet Rnd 6, alternating between 1 row with 13 motifs and 1 row with 14 motifs, off-setting the motifs as shown in the photo. You will have 8 rows with 14 motifs and 7 rows with 13 motifs. Join the Circles together through the ch loops (see page 77).

Finishing

Edging

Rnd 1: Join White to a corner in a ch-sp, ch 7 (= 1 dc plus ch 6), *1 dc in next ch-sp, ch 6; rep from * around, working only 3 ch between motifs, join with sl st to first ch.
Rnd 2: Ch 2 (= 1 dc plus ch 1), 1 sl st in next ch-sp, (1 dc, 1 htr, 3 tr, 1 htr, 1 dc) in each 6-ch sp and 3 dc in each 3 ch-sp around; join with sl st into first dc.
Dampen and dry flat to block.

> **My Tip for You**
> ---
> For an even warmer, cuddlier blanket, attach a lining of fleece fabric to the back of the piece.

You can make this pillow any size by changing the number of Hexagons.

Cuddly Pillow

a splash of color for the home

INTERMEDIATE

FINISHED
MEASUREMENTS
Approx. 40 x 35 cm /
15¾ x 13¾ in

YARN
CYCA #2, Schachenmayr
Original Catania or
equivalent (125 m/
137 yd/ 50 g; 100%
cotton).

YARN AMOUNTS
Orchid 222, Apple 205,
White 106, and Light
Blue 173, 100 g each
Red 115, 50 g

HOOK
3 mm / U.S. sizes C-2/D-3

NOTIONS
Tapestry needle, pillow
form approx. 40 x 35 cm /
15¾ x 13¾ in

GAUGE
20 dc and 24 rows =
10 x 10 cm / 4 x 4 in

Instructions

Make 32 Hexagons (see page 10), working Rnd
1 in Red, Rnd 2 in Orchid, Rnd 3 in Apple, Rnd
4 in White, and Rnd 5 in Light Blue.
Arrange the Hexagons with right sides together as shown in the schematic, and sew them together with Light Blue (see page 77). On the
back of the pillow, leave an opening to turn the
cover right side out.

Finishing

Insert the pillow form and sew the opening
closed using Light Blue.

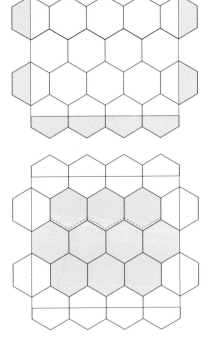

Chic Makeup Bag

plenty of space for creams and such

INTERMEDIATE

FINISHED MEASUREMENTS
Circumference
approx. 18 cm / 7 in
Height approx. 20 cm / 7¾ in

YARN
CYCA #2, Schachenmayr Original Catania or equivalent (125 m/ 137 yd/ 50 g; 100% cotton).

YARN AMOUNTS
Pool 165, 100 g
Taupe 254, 50 g

HOOK
3 mm / U.S. size C-2/D-3

NOTIONS
Tapestry needle, cotton fabric in dark brown (80 x 20 cm / 31½ x 7¾ in), cotton fabric in turquoise (80 x 20 cm / 31½ x 7¾ in), sewing machine, sewing thread in dark brown

GAUGE
20 dc and 24 rows = 10 x 10 cm / 4 x 4 in

Instructions

Make 19 Small Stars (see page 15), working Rnds 1 and 2 with Taupe and Rnds 3 and 4 with Pool. Beginning with 2nd Star, using the schematic as a guide, join the motifs together when working Rnd 4 (see page 77).

Edge
Rnd 1: Join Taupe with sl st in the ch-sp at the top of a star, 1 dc in the same ch-sp, 1 htr in each of next 2 sts, 1 tr in each of next 2 sts, 1 dtr in each of next 8 sts, 1 tr in next 2 sts, 1 htr in next 2 sts, *1 dc in next ch-sp, 1 htr in each of next 2 sts, 1 tr in next 2 sts, 1 dtr in each of next 8 sts, 1 tr in next 2 sts, 1 htr in next 2 sts; rep from * 4 more times; join with sl st in first dc.
Rnd 2: Ch 1, 1 dc in the same st, 1 dc in next 2 htr, 1 htr in next 2 tr, 1 tr in next 8 dtr, 1 htr in next 2 tr, 1 dc in next 2 htr, * 1 dc in the next dc, 1 dc in the next 2 htr, 1 htr in next 2 tr, 1 tr in next 8 dtr, 1 htr in next 2 tr, 1 dc in next 2 htr; rep from * 4 more times; join with sl st in first dc.
Rnd 3: Ch 4 (= 1 tr plus ch 1), sk 1, *1 tr in next st, ch 1, sk 1; rep from * around; join with sl st in 3rd ch.
Rnd 4: Ch 1, sk 2, 5 tr in next 2 sts, sk 2, *1 dc in next st, sk 2, 5 tr in next st, sk 2; rep from * around; join with sl st in first ch.

Lining
With the brown fabric, cut out a rectangle of 56 x 20 cm / 22 x 7¾ in and a circle with a diameter of 17 cm / 6¾ in, including a 1 cm / ³/8 in seam al-lowance. Pin the short sides of the rectangle to-gether to form a tube and sew with a 1 cm / ³/8 in seam allowance. Insert the circle and pin in place at the bottom of the tube. Sew around with a 1 cm / ³/8 in seam allowance. Repeat with the tur-quoise fabric.

With wrong sides together, insert one lining piece inside the other and sew the opening to-gether with a 1 cm / ³/8 in seam allowance, leav-ing an opening of about 8 cm / 3 in to turn the lining right side out. Turn and close the opening with hand stitching. Insert the lining into the bag and blind stitch it on the 3rd round of crochet from the top of the bag.

Finishing

With Pool, cut 4 strands, each 6 m / 6 yd long, and make a twisted cord approx. 80 cm / 32 in long. Knot ends firmly. Weave the cord through Rnd 3 of the bag edging.
Make 4 Small Circles with Taupe:
Make a magic ring (see page 74).
Rnd 1: Ch 1, 6 dc in ring; join with sl st in first dc.
Rnd 2: Ch 2 (= 1 htr), 1 htr in the same st, work 2 htr in each sc around; join with sl st in top of ch. Place the end of the drawstring cord between 2 Small Circles and use Taupe to sew them togeth-er around the knot at the end of the cord. Rep on other end of cord.

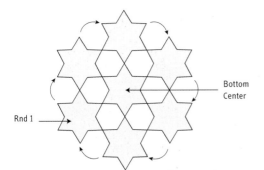

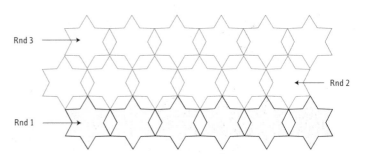

Pastel Loop-Scarf

just so cozy

EASY

SIZE
Adult

FINISHED MEASUREMENTS
Width approx. 76 cm / 30 in

Height approx. 48 cm / 19 in

YARN
CYCA #4, Schachen-mayr Original Favorito or equiva-lent (104 m/ 114 yd/ 50 g; 41% cotton, 34% acrylic, 25% nylon).

YARN AMOUNTS
White 01, 150 g

Taupe 10, 200 g

Mint 72, 50 g

HOOK
5 mm / U.S. size H-8

NOTIONS
Tapestry needle

GAUGE
18 dc and 24 rows = 10 x 10 cm / 4 x 4 in

Instructions

Work 12 Basic Triangles (see page 8 for pattern and below for color sequence) with an additional rnd as follows:

Rnd 6: Ch 3 (= 1 tr), ch 1, *(4 tr, ch 2, 4 tr) in next ch-sp, ch 1 (4 tr, ch 1) in each of the next 4 ch-spaces; rep from * once more, (4 tr, ch 2, 4 tr) in next ch-sp, ch 1, (4 tr, ch 1) in each of the next 3 ch-spaces, 3 tr in next ch-sp; join with sl st in 3rd ch.

• Make 6 Triangles with Rnds 1 and 2 worked in Taupe, Rnd 3 in Mint, Rnd 4 in White, and Rnds 5 and 6 in Taupe.
• Make 6 Triangles with Rnds 1 and 2 worked in White, Rnd 3 in Mint, Rnd 4 in Taupe, and Rnds 5 and 6 in White.

Arrange the Triangles as shown in the schematic and sew them together (see page 77), working loosely. Join the ends to form a loop.

Finishing

The edges are worked in the round.

Edging

Rnd 1: Join Taupe with sl st to a ch-sp at the top of one of the Triangles with Rnd 6 worked in Taupe, ch 4 (= 1 dtr), 3 dtr in the same ch-sp, ch 1, 4 tr in the corner ch-sp of the next White Trian-gle, (ch 1, 4 tr, ch 1) in each of the next 5 ch-spac-es, ch 1, 4 tr in the end corner of the White Trian-gle, ch 1, *4 tr in the top of the next Taupe Triangle, ch 1, 4 tr in the corner ch-sp of the next White Triangle, (ch 1, 4 tr, ch 1) in each of the next 5 ch-spaces, ch 1, 4 tr in the end corner of the White Triangle, ch 1; rep from * once more, join with sl st in 4th ch.

Rnd 2: Ch 3 (=1 tr), (4 tr, ch 1) in each ch-sp around; in the last ch-sp, only work 3 tr, join with sl st in 3rd ch.

Rnd 3: Ch 3 (= 1 tr), 3 tr in first ch-sp, 4 tr in each ch-sp around (and do not make a ch-sp between each group of 4 tr), join with sl st in 3rd ch.

Repeat edging on other side of scarf.

Weave in ends, dampen, and dry flat to block.

Matching Arm Warmers
cuddly comfort

EASY

SIZE
One size fits all

FINISHED MEASUREMENTS
Circumference approx. 26 cm / 10¼ in

Length approx. 28 cm / 11 in

YARN
CYCA #4, Schachenmayr Original Favorito or equivalent (104 m/ 114 yd/ 50 g; 41% cotton, 34% acrylic, 25% nylon).

YARN AMOUNTS
White 01, Taupe 10, and Mint 72, 50 g each

HOOK
5 mm / U.S. size H-8

NOTIONS
Tapestry needle

GAUGE
18 dc and 24 rows = 10 x 10 cm / 4 x 4 in

Instructions

Work 4 Basic Triangles (see page 8 for pattern and below for color sequence) with an additional rnd as follows:

Rnd 6: Ch 3 (= 1 tr), ch 1, *(4 tr, ch 2, 4 tr) in next ch-sp, ch 1 (4 tr, ch 1) in each of the next 4 ch-spaces; rep from * once more, (4 tr, ch 2, 4 tr) in next ch-sp, ch 1, (4 tr, ch 1) in each of the next 3 ch-spaces, 3 tr in next ch-sp, join with sl st in 3rd ch.

• Make 2 Triangles with Rnds 1 and 2 worked in Taupe, Rnd 3 in Mint, Rnd 4 in White, and Rnds 5 and 6 in Taupe.
• Make 2 Triangles with Rnds 1 and 2 worked in White, Rnd 3 in Mint, Rnd 4 in Taupe, and Rnds 5 and 6 in White.

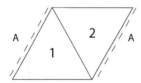

Arrange 2 Triangles (one of each color combination) as shown in the schematic, and sew them together (see page 77). Join the ends to form a loop. Weave in ends.
Repeat for second arm warmer.

My Tip for You

To make smaller arm warmers, just skip Rnd 6 of the Triangles.

Finishing

The edges are worked in the round.

Edging

Rnd 1: Join Taupe with sl st to a ch-sp at the top of one of the Triangles with Rnd 6 worked in Taupe, ch 4 (= 1 dtr), 3 tr in the same ch-sp, 4 tr in the corner ch-sp of the next White Triangle, 4 tr in each of the next 5 ch-spaces, 4 tr in the end corner of the White Triangle, ch 1, join with sl st in 4th ch.

Rnd 2: Ch 3 (= 1 tr), (4 tr) in each ch-sp around (do not make a ch-sp between each group of 4 tr); in the last ch-sp, only work 3 tr; join with sl st in 3rd ch.

Repeat on other edge of arm warmer and on both edges of second arm warmer.

Weave in ends, dampen, and dry flat to block.

Trendy in the Office
delightful laptop case

ADVANCED

FINISHED MEASUREMENTS
Approx. 30 x 25 cm / 11¾ x 9¾ in

YARN
CYCA #2, Schachenmayr Original Catania or equivalent (125 m/ 137 yd/ 50 g; 100% cotton).

YARN AMOUNTS
Raffia 257 and White 106, 100 g each

Light Blue 173, Light Green 260, and Rose 246, 50 g each

HOOK
3 mm / U.S. size C-2/D-3

NOTIONS
Tapestry needle, thick wool felt in camel color 32 x 54 cm / 12½ x 21¼ in, matching sewing thread, washable marking pen, wooden button approx. 3 cm / 1 in diameter

GAUGE
20 dc and 24 rows = 10 x 10 cm / 4 x 4 in

Instructions

Make 28 Hexagon Flowers (see page 10) in the following colors:
- Make 14 with Rnd 1 worked in Rose, Rnd 2 in White, and Rnd 3 in Raffia.
- Make 7 with Rnd 1 worked in Rose, Rnd 2 in White, and Rnd 3 in Light Green.
- Make 7 with Rnd 1 worked in Rose, Rnd 2 in White, and Rnd 3 in Light Blue.

Arrange the motifs as shown in the schematic and sew them together (see page 77) using Raffia yarn.

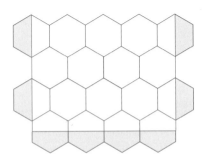

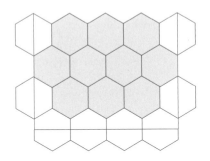

My Tip for You

By adding or removing Hexagon Flowers, you can make this bag to fit any laptop. Keep in mind that the bag should be at least 5 cm / 2 in wider than your computer. Measure the width of the felt to match your bag and add 1 cm / 3/8 in seam allowance. To calculate how much felt you need, measure the length of the bag and multiply by 2 (for the front and back) and then add 10 cm / 4 in for the flap.

Lining

Following the schematic, fold the fabric so it is the height of the bag and sew the side seams with a 0.5 cm / ¼ in seam allowance. Insert the lining into the bag and hand-stitch it in place around the opening of the bag with matching thread.

Some of the fabric will be sticking out of the top of the bag. This will form the flap. Using the template, outline the shape of the flap with the marking pen and cut. With Light Green, work blanket stitch around the edge of the flap. To ensure that the blanket stitch is worked evenly, mark dots along the edge of the flap 1 cm / 3/8 in from the edge and 1 cm / 3/8 in apart. Join Light Green with sl st in the first loop of the blanket stitch. Ch 1, 2 dc in same loop, 3 dc in each loop around edge of flap to the center, ch 15, sl st in the first ch, ch 15 to form a button loop, then work 3 dc in each blanket stitch loop to end of flap. Fasten off and weave in ends.

To reinforce the button loop, join Light Green with a sl st in the 6th dc before the loop, dc in each of the next 5 dc, work 20 dc in the button loop, dc in the next 5 dc on the flap, sl st in next dc, fasten off and weave in end.

Finishing

Using Light Green, sew the button to the center front of the bag approx. 1 cm / 3/8 in below the center of the flap. Make a crochet chain button loop.

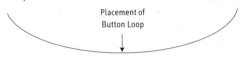
Placement of Button Loop

Note: Enlarge the diagram by 500% to use it as a guide.

Handy-Dandy Keychain

never lose your keys again

EASY

FINISHED MEASUREMENTS
Approx. 18 x 8 cm / 7 x 3 in

YARN
CYCA #2, Schachenmayr Original Catania or equivalent (125 m/ 137 yd/ 50 g; 100% cotton).

YARN AMOUNTS
Small amounts of Natural 105, Light Green 260, Lilac 226, Stone 242, and Silver 172

HOOK
3 mm / U.S. size C-2/D-3

NOTIONS
Tapestry needle, metal carabiner with key ring 2.5 cm / 1 in and 6.5 cm / 2½ in long, metal key ring 2.5 cm / 1 in, cotton gingham check fabric in green and iron-on interfacing 30 x 6 cm / 11¾ x 2½ in, sewing thread in Lilac

GAUGE
20 dc and 24 rows = 10 x 10 cm / 4 x 4 in with smaller hook

Instructions

Make 2 Pentagon with Flower motifs (see page 16), working Rnd 1 in Natural, Rnd 2 in Lilac, Rnds 3 and 4 in Light Green, Rnd 5 in Stone, and Rnd 6 in Silver.

Mini Blossoms
(Make 2)
Make a magic ring (see page 74).
Rnd 1: *Ch 2, 1 tr, ch 2, sl st in the ring; rep from * 4 more times.

Band
Iron the interfacing to the wrong side of the fabric. Double-fold the strip lengthwise, right sides together, and sew with a 0.5 cm / ¼ in seam allowance on the long side. Press the seam. Pull the fabric through the ring and fold in half. Sew the short ends together with a few stitches.

Finishing

With wrong sides facing, line up the two Pentagons and sew them together with Silver yarn (see page 77). Slip the end of the fabric strip in between the two motifs and finish sewing the motifs together, stitching through the fabric. Sew the Mini Blossoms to the fabric with lilac thread.

My Tip for You

If you prefer, you can crochet the band. With Light Green, ch 7, dc in 2nd ch from hook and in each ch across—6 dc. Ch 1, turn, dc in each c and repeat until band is approx. 12 in / 30 cm long.

This neutral-colored headband will go with any outfit. If you prefer something brighter, choose your favorite colors.

Granny-style Headband
in neutral hues

EASY

SIZE
One size fits all

FINISHED MEASUREMENTS
Approx. 50 x 9 cm / 19½ x 3½ in

YARN
Shown: CYCA #3, Schachenmayr SMC Extra Merino or equivalent (130 m/ 142 yd/ 50 g; 100% cotton).

YARN AMOUNTS
Beige Heather 03 and Bark Heather 12, 50 g each

SUBSTITUTION
Schachenmayr Original Merino Extra Fine (120 m / 132 yd / 50 g). Available Fall 2014

HOOK
4 mm / U.S. size G-6

NOTIONS
Tapestry needle

GAUGE
22 dc and 30 rows = 10 x 10 cm / 4 x 4 in

Instructions

Make 4 Rectangles (see page 14), working Rnd 1 in Bark, Rnd 2 in Beige, and Rnd 3 in Bark. Join the short sides of the rectangles (see page 77) end to end to form a ring.

Finishing

Edging

Rnd 1: Join Beige Heather with sl st in a ch-sp, ch 1, 1 dc in each tr and 1-ch space; work 2 dc in the corner of each rectangle; join with sl st in first ch.
Rnd 2: Ch 3 (= 1 tr), 1 tr in first ch, sk 2, dc in next st, *ch 3, tr in the front 2 loops of the last dc, sk 2; rep from * around. Join with sl st in beg ch.
Repeat on other side of ring.

The clusters give the flowers a puffy appearance. Because this rug is worked with a double strand of yarn, it is extra soft.

Blossom Rug

fantastically soft on the toes

INTERMEDIATE

FINISHED MEASUREMENTS
Approx. 100 x 90 cm / 39½ x 36½ in

YARN
Shown: CYCA #4, Schachenmayr SMC Cotton Time or equivalent (98 m/ 96 yd/ 50 g; 100% cotton).

YARN AMOUNTS
Graphite 98, 500 g
Black 99, 300 g
White 01, 200 g
Lavender 46, 100 g

SUBSTITUTION
Schachenmayr Original Sun City (95 m / 106 yd / 50 g).

HOOK
8 mm / U.S. size L-11

NOTIONS
Tapestry needle

GAUGE
20 dc and 25 rows = 10 x 10 cm / 4 x 4 in with a single strand of yarn and size 3.5 mm / U.S. size E-4 hook.

Instructions

With 2 strands held together (using 2 separate balls of yarn), make 19 Circle with Flower motifs (see page 11), working Rnd 1 in Lavender, Rnd 2 in White, Rnd 3 in Black, and Rnd 4 in Graphite.

Arrange the motifs as shown in the schematic to form a hexagon. With Graphite, join the motifs together (see page 77), working 6 sts on each piece at the joins.

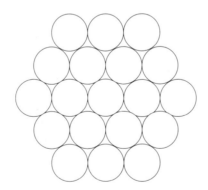

Finishing

Edging (worked around)

Rnd 1: Join Graphite with sl st to a ch-sp, ch 3 (= 1 tr), 1 tr in same ch-sp, work 1 tr in each cluster and 2 tr in each ch-sp around, and, at the transitions between motifs, do not crochet between the motifs, but leave a gap (see photo); join with sl st to top of beg ch.

Rnd 2: Ch 3, tr in same tr, 1 tr in each tr around, working the last 3 sts and the first 3 sts of each motif together as a decrease; join with sl st to top of beg ch.

Fasten off.

Elegant Placemats

stylishly decorated table

EASY

FINISHED MEASUREMENTS
Approx. 50 x 35 cm /
19 ½ x 13 ¾ in

YARN
CYCA #2, Schachenmayr
Original Catania or
equivalent (125 m/ 137
yd/ 50 g; 100%
cotton).

YARN AMOUNTS
Pale Green 262, Pearl
255, Fuchsia 128, and
Rose 246, 50 g each

HOOK
3 mm / U.S. size C-2/D-3

NOTIONS
Tapestry needle, straight
pins or washable mark-
ing pen, 2 pink place-
mats, embroidery needle

GAUGE
20 dc and 24 rows =
10 x 10 cm / 4 x 4 in

Instructions

Make 4 Paisleys (see page 13), working Rnd 1
in Rose, Rnds 2 and 3 in Fuchsia, Rnd 4 in
Pearl, Rnd 5 in Pale Green, and Rnd 6 in Pearl.
Weave in ends, dampen motifs, and dry flat to
block.

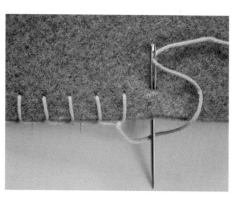

Use pins or washable marker to mark evenly
spaced locations across each end of the placemats. Using Pale Green, work Blanket Stitch
embroidery on ends of placemats (see photo).

Finishing

Pin the motifs onto the placemats in the desired locations, and then stitch in place by
hand with Fuchsia on Rnd 2 and Pale Green on
Rnd 6.

These potholders have extra insulation from heat because they are made with a double layer of crochet.

Chic Potholders
for star chefs

INTERMEDIATE

FINISHED MEASUREMENTS
Approx. 20 x 20 cm / 8 x 8 in

YARN
CYCA #2, Schachenmayr Original Catania or equivalent (125 m/ 137 yd/ 50 g; 100% cotton).

YARN AMOUNTS
Small amounts of White 106, Jeans 164, Light Blue 173, and Red Wine 192

HOOK
2.5 mm / U.S. size B-1/C-2

NOTIONS
Tapestry needle

GAUGE
26 dc and 36 rows = 10 x 10 cm / 4 x 4 in

Instructions

Make 4 Five-Point Stars (see page 11) in the following colors:
- Make 2 with Rnds 1-4 worked in White, Rnd 5 in Jeans, Rrnd 6 in Red Wine, and Rnds 7-9 in Light Blue.
- Make 2 with Rnds 1-4 worked in White, Rnd 5 in Red Wine, Rnd 6 in Light Blue, and Rnds 7-9 in Jeans.

Weave in ends, wash motifs, and dry flat to block.

Finishing

Place 2 motifs of the same colors together with right sides facing out. The border is worked through the edges of both motifs together to make a double-thick fabric.

Rnd 1: Join White with a sl st in a ch-sp, 2 dc in same ch-sp, 1 dc in each dc around, working 3 dc in each corner ch-sp, and, in the last corner, work (2 dc, ch 15, sl st in first ch, 1 dc; join with sl st in first ch.

Rnd 2: Ch 1, 2 dc in next st, 1 dc in each dc working 2 dc in the middle stitch of each corner, and 20 dc around loop; join with sl st in first ch.

Alphabet Banner
perfect for parties

EASY

FINISHED MEASUREMENTS
Approx. 140 x 23 cm /
55 x 9 in

YARN
CYCA #2, Schachenmayr
Original Catania or
equivalent (125 m/
137 yd/ 50 g; 100%
cotton).

YARN AMOUNTS
Light Green 260, Rose
246, Pool 165, Sun 208,
50 g each

Small amounts of Freesia
251, Apple 205, Peacock
146, Mandarin Orange
209, and White 106

HOOK
3 mm / U.S. size C-2/D-3

NOTIONS
Tapestry needle, natural
wool felt, amount
depending on the length
of the name, embroidery
needle, orange embroi-
dery yarn

GAUGE
20 dc and 24 rows =
10 x 10 cm / 4 x 4 in

Instructions

Make one Easy Triangle (see page 12) for each letter in the name you've chosen, working Rnds 1-5 in lighter color with Rnd 6 in corresponding darker color: pair Light Green and Apple, Sun and Mandarin, Rose and Freesia, and Pool and Peacock.

Note: Vary the colors of your Triangles for the best effect. For example, a name with 8 letters should have two Triangles of each color.

Work additional border along 2 sides of triangle:
Next row: Join corresponding darker color to corner with sl st, ch 4, sk 1, sl st in next st, *ch 3, sk 1, sl st in next st; rep from * across 2 sides to the 1st dc of the 2nd corner; work 2 dc in bottom corner of triangle. Fasten off. Weave in ends. Wash motifs and dry flat to block.

Letters
Cut desired letters out of paper, trace them onto felt, and cut them out. Arrange the letters on the Triangles with pins and sew in place by hand, using a running stitch to outline the letter.

Chain
Arrange Triangles in order, spelling out the name you've chosen. Starting with last letter, and working to first letter from right to left, join Triangles with White: Ch 80, *sl st in the right-most ch-sp of the last Triangle in the row; working in the back loops only, sl st in each dc along the Triangle; sl st in the ch-sp at the left corner of the triangle, ch 10; rep from * across all triangles, ch 70. Turn and sl st in each st across. Fasten off and weave in ends.

Tassels
Wrap yarn 30 times around a postcard or box that is about 7 cm / 2¾ in long. Tie a knot around the top of the tassel. Remove the yarn from the postcard or box, and tie off with a piece of yarn approx. 2 cm / ¾ in from the top. Cut the bottom of the tassel open.

Finishing

Attach a tassel to the bottom point of each Triangle.

This pincushion is super practical and pretty all at the same time. It makes a perfect small project for a gift.

Pincushion with a Difference
the natural look

EASY

FINISHED MEASUREMENTS
Approx. 12 cm / 4½ in circumference

YARN
CYCA #2, Schachen-mayr Original Catania or equiva-lent (125 m/ 137 yd/ 50 g; 100% cotton).

YARN AMOUNTS
Small amounts of Natural 105, Linen 248, Rose 246, and Freesia 251

HOOK
3 mm / U.S. sizes C-2/D-3

NOTIONS
Tapestry needle, lin-en fabric 12 x 6 in / 30 x 15 cm, fiber fill approx. 30 g, sewing needle and matching thread

GAUGE
20 dc and 24 rows = 10 x 10 cm / 4 x 4 in

Instructions

Make 2 Circles with Flowers (see page 15), working Rnd 1 in Rose, Rnd 2 in Natural, Rnd 3 in Freesia, Rnd 4 in Rose, Rnd 5 in Linen, Rnd 6 in Rose, and Rnd 7 in Natural.

Stuffing
Fold the linen in half and cut out two 12 cm / 4½ in circles using a CD as a guide. Sew the pieces together with a 0.5 cm / ¼ in seam al-lowance, leaving a 3 cm / 1¼ in opening for turning right side out. Turn right side out, stuff with fiber-fill, and hand-sew opening closed.

Finishing

With right sides facing out, hold both Circles together and, working through both layers, dc halfway around the edges. Place the stuffed cushion between the Circles and work dc around to the beginning. Join with sl st in first dc.

Felted Bag
in cheerful colors

INTERMEDIATE

FINISHED MEASUREMENTS
Before felting approx. 45 cm / 17¾ in wide and 37 cm / 14½ in long

YARN
Shown: CYCA #4, Schachenmayr SMC Wash+Filz-it! Fine or equivalent (100 m/ 109 yd/ 50 g; 100% wool).

YARN AMOUNTS
Violet 118, 100 g

Plum 126, Pink 11, and White 102, 50 g each

SUBSTITUTION
Istex Léttlopi (100 m/ 109 yd / 50 g).

HOOKS
4.5 mm and 8 mm / U.S. sizes 7 and L-11

NOTIONS
Tapestry needle, pompom maker or two 5 cm / 2 in cardboard stencils, magnetic button 18 mm / ¾ in, a few yards of pearl cotton embroidery thread in matching color, 2 tennis balls and several plastic grocery bags (for felting)

GAUGE
16 tr and 22 rows = 10 x 10 cm / 4 x 4 in with smaller hook

Instructions

With smaller hook, make 22 Diamonds (see page 17) with White, Pink, Plum, and Violet. Arrange the motifs as shown in the schematic. With a double-strand of Violet and larger hook, work 2 dc in each ch-sp (between the tr of final rnd of motif), and 3 dc in each corner at the top of a diamond ch-sp, and dc2tog in the dip between diamonds.

Handles

With Violet, work the handles in Cord Stitch (see below), using two strands of yarn held together and larger hook. Make each handle approx. 22 cm / 8½ in long and sew them to the top corners of the diamonds.

Cord Stitch

Ch 3, insert the hook into the outer loop of the second chain and draw up a loop. Insert the hook into the outer edge of the first chain and draw up a loop, yarn around hook, draw yarn through all

3 loops on the hook. Turn and work 1 dc in each of the the two loops on the side. Rep from * until cord is desired length.

Ties

With Violet, make three thinner cords as foll: Ch 26 (21, 16), turn, sl st in second chain and each chain to end. Tie a piece of pearl cotton to the end of the cord.

Pompoms

Make 3 pompoms, 1 in each of the darker colors. Use the pearl cotton at the end of the ties to attach the pompoms. Sew the other ends of the cords to the upper edge of the bag.

Finishing

Put the bag in the washing machine with 2 tennis balls and run through the regular wash cycle with hot water. When the bag has felted, immediately remove it from the washer, shape as desired, stuff with plastic bags, and allow to dry completely.
Attach a magnetic button to the inside of the bag opening with the pearl cotton.

My Tip for You

Using a double strand of yarn and a large crochet hook, you can make a very thick, round handle. But this may be difficult for beginners, so practice first with a single strand of yarn and a smaller hook.

Corner | Dip

Middle

29 in / 74 cm

17¾ in / 45 cm

Note: 22 diamonds. Arrows indicate the motifs that are joined together.

Colorful Hacky Sack Balls in No Time
great for juggling or kicking

EASY

FINISHED MEASUREMENTS
Approx. 8.5 cm / 3¼ in

YARN
CYCA #2, Schachenmayr Original Catania or equivalent (125 m/ 137 yd/ 50 g; 100% cotton).

YARN AMOUNTS
Small amounts of Linen 248, Apricot 263, Camilla 252, Strawberry 258, and Taupe 254

HOOK
3 mm / U.S. size C-2/D-3

NOTIONS
Tapestry needle, fiberfill

GAUGE
6 tr and 36 rows = 10 x 10 cm / 4 x 4 in

Instructions

For each ball, make 12 Easy Pentagons (see page 17) in the colors shown on the schematics.

Group 1

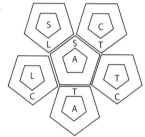

Group 2

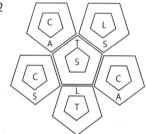

A = Apricot
S = Strawberry
C = Camilla
L = Linen
T = Taupe

1. Join Group 1 motifs to all sides of a central Pentagon.
2. Join Group 2 motifs to all sides of a central Pentagon.
3. Join remaining motifs of Group 1 and Group 2 together. Stuff with fiberfill before joining final 2-3 seams.

Finishing

With any color, join (see page 77) 6 motifs following Group 1 schematic and 6 motifs following Group 2 schematic. Join remaining sides of motifs, stuffing with fiberfill before closing final 2-3 seams.
Bury the ends inside the balls.

Eye-catching Cell Phone Case

protective cover

EASY

FINISHED MEASUREMENTS
Approx. 12.5 x 8 cm / 5 x 3 in

YARN
CYCA #2, Schachenmayr Original Catania Fine or equivalent (125 m/ 137 yd / 50 g; 100% cotton).

YARN AMOUNTS
Eggplant 1006, Jade 1020, and Linen 1009, 50 g each

HOOK
3 mm / U.S. size C-2/D-3

NOTIONS
Tapestry needle

GAUGE
28 tr and 36 rows = 10 x 10 cm / 4 x 4 in

Instructions

Make 7 Triangles (see page 17) with Eggplant, Jade, and Linen.
Make 2 Dots (see page 17) in Eggplant.
With Eggplant, loosely crochet the Triangles together (see page 77) as shown in the schematic, working the join between two Triangles as follows: 2 sc in a 3-ch sp, ch 3, sk 4 dc, 2 dc in sp between dc groups, ch 3, sk 4 dc, 2 dc in sp between dc groups, ch 3, sk 4 dc, 2 sc in 3-ch sp.

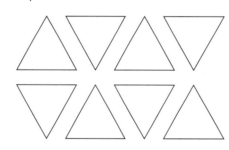

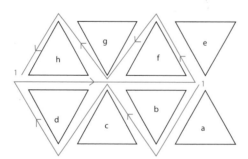

Form into a loop to complete case:
Join h to e and d to a.

Finishing

Join the Dots in the center of the front and back in the same manner. Work border around top opening with Eggplant, working 1 sc in each ch-sp and ch 4 over each dc group.

Upholstered Stool

with bright blue flowers

EXPERIENCED

FINISHED MEASUREMENTS
Approx. 28 x 28 cm /
11 x 11 in

YARN
CYCA #2, Schachenmayr
Original Catania or
equivalent (125 m/ 137
yd/ 50 g; 100%
cotton).

YARN AMOUNTS
Pearl 255, Light Blue
173, Cloud 247, and
Hyacinth 240, approx.
50 g each

HOOK
3 mm / U.S. size C-2/D-3

NOTIONS
Tapestry needle

GAUGE
26 tr and 36 rows =
10 x 10 cm / 4 x 4 in

Instructions

Make 19 Radiant Blossoms (see page 17) with
Pearl, Light Blue, Cloud, and Hyacinth.
Make 24 Mini Circles (see page 17) in Cloud.
Arrange the motifs as shown in the schematic
and use Hyacinth to join with dc on wrong
sides (see page 77).

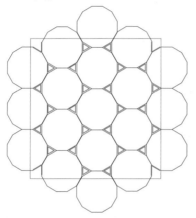

▷ = Mini Circle
⌐ = Joining Crochet

To avoid having too many ends to weave in,
sl st to the point where the next seam begins,
then continue to join motifs. In each corner,
attach 2 additional Radiant Blossom motifs.

Finishing

Weave in ends.
Make 2 chains approx. 100 cm / 40 in long.
Weave one chain around the edge of the piece
and, starting in the opposite corner, weave the
second approx. 0.5 cm / ¼ in away from the
first. Place the covering over the stool and
gather in the chains. Tie the ends of the cords
together to fasten.

Original Cushion

not a square

EXPERIENCED

FINISHED MEASUREMENTS
Approx. 48 cm / 18¾ in circumference

YARN
CYCA #2, Schachen-mayr Original Catania or equivalent (125 m/ 137 yd/ 50 g; 100% cotton).

YARN AMOUNTS
Raffia 257, 200 g

Gold 249, Lilac 226, and Hyacinth 240, 50 g each

HOOK
3 mm / U.S. size C-2/D-3

NOTIONS
Tapestry needle, 12 buttons in lilac approx. 15 mm/ ½ in, cotton fabric in beige 50 x 50 cm / 20 x 20 in, fiberfill 500 g, sewing machine, sewing thread in matching color

GAUGE
26 tr and 36 rows = 10 x 10 cm / 4 x 4 in

Instructions

Make 50 Propeller motifs (see page 18) in the following colors:

- 14 in Gold and Raffia
- 24 in Lilac and Raffia
- 12 in Hyacinth and Raffia

Make 6 Squares (see page 18) in Hyacinth and Raffia for the side.

Arrange the motifs as shown in Schematics 1 and 2 and join with dc (see page 77), working into 1 ch-sp, 7 tr, and 1 ch-sp on the edge of each Propeller motif. While joining the back, leave an opening as shown. Work sc around the opening, working 2 dc and 2 ch in each corner on the bottom of the opening for button loops. Along the top of the opening, attach 6 buttons as shown on the diagram, matching the locations of the button loops. Sew on the second set of 6 buttons as shown on the diagram, for decoration; there is no second opening. Weave in ends and press on the WS.

Finishing

Fold the cotton fabric in half, right sides together. Using the pillowcase as a guide, cut out two hexagons with a 1 cm / ³/8 in seam allowance. Sew the pieces of fabric together, leaving an opening to turn right side out. Turn right side out, stuff with fiberfill, and close the opening. Insert the pillow into the crochet pillow case.

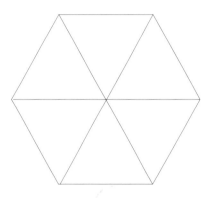

If you enlarge this template so the diagonals measure 48 cm / 19 in, you can use this as a pattern to cut the cotton fabric.

Schematic 1: Back

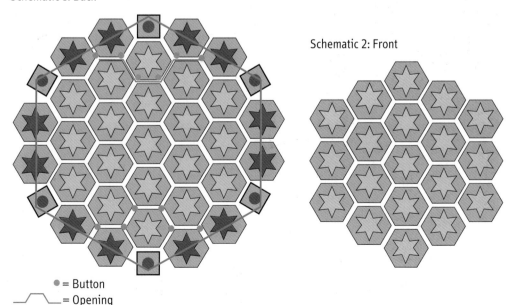

Schematic 2: Front

● = Button

‿‿ = Opening

It's easy to dream with the bright shining stars on this lampshade. When the light is on, it casts decorative shadows.

  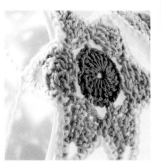

Table Lamp with Glowing Stars

for a heavenly atmosphere

INTERMEDIATE

FINISHED MEASUREMENTS
Circumference approx.
14 cm / 5½ in
Height approx.
19 cm / 7½ in

YARN
CYCA #2, Schachenmayr Original Catania Fine or equivalent (125 m/ 137 yd/ 50 g; 100% cotton).

YARN AMOUNTS
Gray 1019, Light Blue 1015, and White 1000, 50 g each

HOOK
2.5 mm/ U.S. size B-1/C-2

NOTIONS
Tapestry needle, lamp-shade circumference 14 cm / 5½ in and 24.5 cm/ 9½ in tall

GAUGE
28 tr and 36 rows =
10 x 10 cm/ 4 x 4 in

Instructions

Make 15 Stars (see page 18), working in rows and joining with sl st.
The numbers on the diagram show the order for crocheting the Stars. Connect the motifs at the tips of the Stars by replacing the ch 2 of tip with 1 sl st for the connection. Connect Stars 13, 14, and 15 with Stars 1, 2, and 3 to form a ring.
Weave in ends.

Finishing

When all of the motifs are complete and joined into a ring, place the piece over the lampshade. Cut two strands of White approx. 80 cm/ 31½ in long. Thread one through the edge of the crochet on the top of the shade and gather it in to fit, and use the other on the bottom of the shade. Knot the ends to secure.

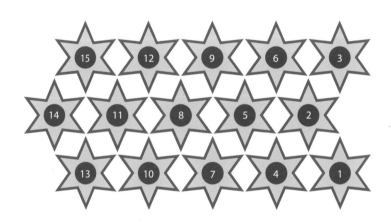

Practical Pouch

pens, pencils, markers—neatly stowed away

INTERMEDIATE

FINISHED MEASUREMENTS
Approx. 7 x 21 cm / 2¾ x 8½ in

YARN
CYCA #2, Schachenmayr Original Catania or equivalent (125 m/ 137 yd/ 50 g; 100% cotton).

YARN AMOUNTS
Natural 105, Linen 248, and Willow 250, 50 g each

HOOK
3 mm / U.S. size C-2/D-3

NOTIONS
Tapestry needle, 2 beads approx. 1 cm / ³/8 in

GAUGE
26 tr and 36 rows = 10 x 10 cm / 4 x 4 in

My Tip for You

A crocheted cord can be used to effectively close the pouch. Making a cord with a double strand of yarn and a large hook can be difficult for a beginner, so practice first with one strand of yarn and a smaller hook.

Instructions

Make 6 Octagons (see page 18) in Willow, Natural, Linen, Willow.
Make 2 Squares (see page 19) in Linen.
Make 4 Triangles (see page 19) in Linen.
Make 2 Pentagons (see page 19) in Linen.

Arrange the motifs as shown in the diagrams and join with dc (see page 77) on the wrong side. Always work a dc in the ch-sp at the corner of each motif; work about 8 or 9 dc on the side of each motif. On the Pentagon, work 2 dc in each corner between the tr sts. On the Octagon, work 2 dc in the corner ch-sp.

Finishing

With Linen and Cord Stitch (see Felted Bag, p. 59, for instructions), crochet a cord approx. 80 cm / 31½ in long, attaching a bead to each end of the chain. Weave the chain through ch-spaces between the Octagons and wrap it around the pouch to secure.

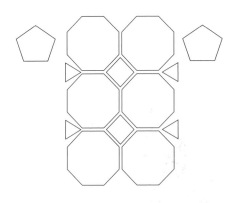

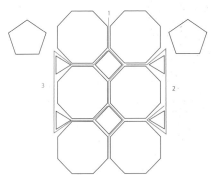

Suggestion for joining: Sew the seams marked in the diagram, and work any remaining seams separately.

A couple of granny coasters sewn onto a solid table cloth make any space colorful.

Flowers in Circles
jazz up any table

INTERMEDIATE

FINISHED MEASUREMENTS
Approx. 9.5 cm / 3¾ in

YARN
CYCA #2, Schachenmayr Original Catania or equivalent (125 m/ 137 yd/ 50 g; 100% cotton).

YARN AMOUNTS
Chartreuse 245, Pool 165, and Taupe 254, 50 g each

HOOK
3 mm / U.S. size C-2/D-3

NOTIONS
Tapestry needle, linen table cloth, sewing machine, matching sewing thread

GAUGE
26 tr and 36 rows = 10 x 10 cm / 4 x 4 in

Instructions

Make 6 Flower in Circle motifs (see page 19) in the following colors:
• 2 with Pool, Chartreuse, Taupe, Pool, Pool, Taupe
• 2 with Taupe, Chartreuse, Taupe, Pool, Taupe, Pool
• 1 with Chartreuse, Taupe, Pool, Chartreuse, Chartreuse, Taupe
• 1 with Pool, Chartreuse, Taupe, Pool, Pool, Chartreuse

Finishing

Machine-stitch the motifs onto the table cloth as shown in the photo or as desired. Press on the wrong side.

My Tip for You

You can also use these motifs as coasters. To contrast with the table-cloth, make the center solid by working the first 3 rnds with the same color.

Techniques

ABBREVIATIONS

beg = begin(s)(ning)

ch = chain

cm = centimeter(s)

dc = double crochet (US single crochet)

dtr = double treble (US treble crochet)

htr = half treble crochet (US half
   double crochet)

in = inch(es)

mm = millimeter(s)

rem = remain(s) (ing)

rep = repeat

rnd(s) = round(s)

RS = right side

sk = skip

sl = slip

st(s) = stitch(es)

tog = together

tr = treble (US double crochet)

WS = wrong side

yoh = yarn over hook (US yarnover/yarn
   around hook/yo)

Note: You can save yourself a lot of work by weaving in the ends as you go whenever you change colors. Simply tie the new yarn around the old yarn, lay the tails on the edge of the work, and crochet over them for at least the first 5 stitches of the new round to secure.

Most of the projects in this book are made with treble crochet. However, some projects also use double, half treble, and double treble crochet stitches. To ensure that your crocheting goes smoothly, review the following sections that illustrate the techniques you need to know.

Gauge Swatch

Work a gauge swatch before beginning any crochet project. The swatch allows you to count the number of stitches and rows in a 10 x 10 cm / 4 x 4 in square, worked in the specified stitch. If more than one hook is used in the pattern, the gauge information will tell you what size hook to use for your swatch. For an accurate measurement, make a swatch that measures at least 12 x 12 cm / 4½ x 4½ in. Place the swatch on a flat surface and count the number of stitches and rows in 10 x 10 cm / 4 x 4 in. If your gauge matches that specified in the pattern, use the same size hook for your project. If you have fewer stitches and rows than specified, use a smaller hook. If you have more stitches and rows than specified, use a larger hook.

Beginning with a Chain Ring

First, make a chain with the specified number of stitches. Then, join the chain into a ring by working a slip stitch into the first chain, as follows: insert the hook into the first chain, and draw the yarn through the chain and through the loop on the hook. The beginning and ending chains are now connected.

Beginning with a Magic Ring

Wrap the working yarn twice around your index finger, with the tail in back. Insert the crochet hook into the loop from right to left, and pull the working yarn through. Work into the ring as specified in the pattern. When the project is finished, you can draw the ring closed by gently pulling on the tail; weave in the end on the wrong side of the work.

Double Crochet (dc) (not pictured)

Insert the hook into the next st and draw up a loop. Yarn over hook and draw working yarn through both loops on the hook.

Treble Crochet (tr)

At the beginning of a row or round, chain three (this counts as the first treble crochet). To work the remaining stitches, yarn around hook, and insert the hook into the next stitch.

Pull up a loop. There are now three loops on the hook.

Yarn over and draw yarn through two loops on hook. Two loops remain on the hook.

Yarn over and draw yarn through two loops on hook again. One loop remains on the hook. The photo shows the first and second treble crochet stitches, with the first stitch replaced by the beginning chain.

Half Treble Crochet (htr)

At the beginning of a row or round, chain two (this counts as the first half treble crochet). To work the remaining stitches, yarn around hook, and insert the hook into the next stitch.

Yarn over and draw yarn through all three loops on the hook. One loop remains on the hook. The photo shows the first and second half treble crochet stitches, with the first stitch replaced by the beginning chain.

Back Post Treble Crochet

To work back post crochet stitches, which create a relief pattern on the surface of the fabric, instead of inserting the hook into the top of the next stitch, insert it from right to left behind the body or *post* of the stitch as shown in the photo. Pull the working yarn through and complete the stitch as you would normally.

Double Treble Crochet (dtr)

At the beginning of a row or round, chain four (this counts as the first double treble crochet). To work the remaining stitches, yarn around hook twice, and insert the hook into the next stitch.

Pull up a loop. There are now four loops on the hook.

Yarn over and draw yarn through two loops on hook. Three loops remain on the hook.

Yarn over and draw yarn through two loops on hook again. Two loops remain on the hook.

Yarn over and draw yarn through two loops on hook a third time. One loop remains on the hook. The photo shows the first and second double treble crochet stitches, with the first stitch replaced by the beginning chain.

Joining Motifs in Chain Loops

Work half of the number of chains specified for the loop, slip stitch in the chain loop on the second motif...

...then work the rest of the chain stitches in the loop.

Crochet Seams

Place motifs wrong sides together, and work double crochet through both layers to join motifs, as foll: *Insert the hook through the next stitch on the front piece, then through the next stitch on the back piece and pull up 1 loop, yarn over and draw yarn through both loops on hook. Rep from * along edge to seam.

Insert the hook into a stitch in a corner where two motifs meet.

Work a dc in the next pair of stitches (1 stitch on each motif).

Chain 1. Pull the tail to the wrong side of the work for weaving in later.

Sl st to the stitch at the corner. Pull the yarn tail to the wrong side for weaving in later.

Sewn Seams

Place motifs together with right sides up and sew the back loops together as shown.

Always secure the corners by working in a stitch from all of the adjoining motifs (possibly working twice in the same loops).

Yarn Suppliers

For a list of suppliers, please visit the Search Press website: www.searchpress.com.

If you are unable to obtain any of the yarn used in this book, it can be replaced with a yarn of a similar weight and composition. Please note, however, the finished projects may vary slightly from those shown, depending on the yarn used.

For more information on selecting or substituting yarn contact your local yarn shop or an online store, they are familiar with all types of yarns and would be happy to help you. Additionally, the online knitting community at Ravelry.com has forums where you can post questions about specific yarns. Yarns come and go so quickly these days and there are so many beautiful yarns available.

About the Authors

BÉATRICE SIMON

As a child, Béatrice Simon was charmed by the magic of crochet. It all started with Aunt Lila, who first taught her to make granny squares in the 1970s. Her studies in languages and linguistics led her to travel widely, especially in southern Germany, where she taught her mother tongue for many years and worked as a translator. About six years ago, she decided to focus on translating works about her favorite subject: needlework, in German, English, and French. At the same time, she rediscovered the endless possibilities for creating magic with just a hook and some yarn. In memory of her Aunt Lila, she took the pseudonym "lillicroche," which she uses on her tri-lingual blog, lillicroche.wordpress.com, and published patterns. Since 2009, she has been living in Brittany, France, where the pot of ideas never stops simmering.

THANK YOU!

A special thanks goes out to my two fairies: Francine, my "mom," and Emilie, my Aunt Lila, for everything they taught me.

BARBARA WILDER

Barbara Wilder lives with her husband and two grown children in the Heilbronn district of Germany, just north of Stuttgart. She has loved needlework since she was a little girl. As a child, she spent a lot of time with her grandmother, an accomplished seamstress, who brought many kinds of handwork into her life. It was clear from early on that the granddaughter would follow in her grandmother's footsteps. Barbara Wilder started her own business under the name "Raumseelig" (raumseelig.blogspot.com). Her focus is textile decoration. Recently she began studying graphic design and has a head full of creative ideas waiting to be implemented.

THANK YOU!

My special thanks to my daughter, who helped me with these projects, and my husband, who managed the household in addition to his profession so I could completely devote myself to the projects in this book.